Christian Political Theology in an Age of Discontent

Christian Political Theology in an Age of Discontent

Mediating Scripture, Doctrine, and Political Reality

JONATHAN COLE
Foreword by Carl Raschke

WIPF & STOCK · Eugene, Oregon

CHRISTIAN POLITICAL THEOLOGY IN AN AGE OF DISCONTENT
Mediating Scripture, Doctrine, and Political Reality

Copyright © 2019 Jonathan Cole. All rights reserved. Except for brief quotations in critical publications or reviews, no part of this book may be reproduced in any manner without prior written permission from the publisher. Write: Permissions, Wipf and Stock Publishers, 199 W. 8th Ave., Suite 3, Eugene, OR 97401.

Wipf & Stock
An Imprint of Wipf and Stock Publishers
199 W. 8th Ave., Suite 3
Eugene, OR 97401

www.wipfandstock.com

PAPERBACK ISBN: 978-1-5326-7934-6
HARDCOVER ISBN: 978-1-5326-7935-3
EBOOK ISBN: 978-1-5326-7936-0

Manufactured in the U.S.A.   MAY 15, 2019

*To my father,
for teaching me
to think for myself.*

Contents

Foreword by Carl Raschke / ix
Acknowledgements / xxi
Introduction / xxiii

1. The Challenge for Christian Political Theology / 1
2. The Art of Political Theology / 11
3. Carl Schmitt and the True German Origins of Christian Political Theology / 20
4. The Problematic Greek Roots of Contemporary Christian Political Theology / 30
5. Christian Political Theology and Secular Political Philosophy / 38
6. Reason and Nature / 46
7. "Thank You Lord Jesus for President Trump" / 55
8. The Calvinist Roots of Evangelical Support for President Trump / 61
9. Christianity and the American Conservative Movement / 68
10. The Politics of Jesus and Christian Anarchism / 76
11. Political Anthropology and the Post-Liberal Future / 86
12. In Defense of Politics / 94

Bibliography / 103
Subject Index / 111
Author Index / 117

Foreword

ACADEMIC AND PUBLIC INTEREST in political theology has evolved over the past half century within the shadow of what Jürgen Habermas in the early 1970s termed a "legitimation crisis" for the postmodern liberal order. Unlike the chaos of the Weimar Republic during the 1920s, which inspired the jurist Carl Schmitt to coin the expression "political theology" itself as a means of locating sovereignty not in the outcome of rowdy parliamentary deliberations but in the divine order, it was the social and cultural upheavals of the late 1960s throughout the Western world that thrust the issue to the fore. As the leading heir at the time to the "revisionist" Marxist project of the Frankfurt School, Habermas ascribed this legitimation crisis to what he dubbed the "anonymization of class domination." Contra Marx, Habermas argued, the ruling class no longer requires the state to maintain its dominance. Instead "the now autonomous economic exchange relieves the political order of the pressures of legitimation."[1] In other words, what Friedrich Hayek, the *éminence grise* of neoliberal economics, referred to as the "truth" of the self-regulating market had come in Habermas' view to function in late industrial capitalism as the covert transcendental source of authority for all political valuations in late industrial capitalism.

The legitimacy of the political order, Habermas argued, cannot derive from economic structures and functions, but only from the "socio-cultural" system itself, which capitalism has

---

1. Habermas, *Legitimation Crisis*, 22.

undermined. "The legitimizing system," he contended, "does not succeed in maintaining the requisite level of mass loyalty while the steering imperatives taken over from the economic system are carried through."[2] In succeeding years Habermas sought to offer a solution to the "legitimation crisis" of late capitalism by crafting what he characterized as a "communicative ethic" embedded in the deliberative processes of grass-roots democracy, but the project remained an academic abstraction that never found its way, either in Europe or in America, into the actual policy arena. While Habermas took great pains, with Germany's horrific Nazi legacy unmistakably in mind, to ensure that the principles of legitimation he proposed could not be construed in any manner as having any authoritarian overtones, Schmitt's own reliance on both a "decisionist" and an "exceptionalist" reading of Western political theory within its historical Christian-monarchial framework found a much more avid readership in light of the rapid social transformations, along with the concurrent chaos, that characterized the last part of the twentieth century. Monarchialism (or in its more extreme versions Caesaro-papism) per se as a concrete political model for the restoration of authority in the modern era held little sway, except perhaps among a few cranky reactionaries with little intellectual clout.

But what might be termed its "eschatological" variant of the kind espoused by Walter Benjamin, who melded Marxist materialism with Jewish messianism at the same time Schmitt was writing, came to have a strong cachet in the revolutionary climate of the late 1960s and 70s. Appealing to a certain type of irrefragable "mandate of history" rather than the absolutist claims of a living sovereign, a left-wing passion for a postmodern style of political theology became popular during the latter period. Closely associated with the writings of Protestant theologian Jürgen Moltmann and Catholic thinker Johann Baptist Metz, who both began to use routinely the term "political theology" with connotations Schmitt himself could have never envisaged, this new breed of Christian intellectuals and activists succeeded for a season in aligning religious thought with

2. Habermas, *Legitimation Crisis*, 46.

Foreword

progressive politics in both its mainstream and Marxist forms. Latin American "liberation theology," represented in such figures as Gustavo Gutiérrez and Juan Luis Segundo and conceptually allied with the sort of historicist Marxism hammered out in German universities, also gained prominence during this time. The conservative reaction and collapse of world Communism that decade of the 1980s, together with the neoliberal reorganization of the global economy that followed, brought an end to this "second wave" of political theology. Another factor was the growing popularity of French post-structuralist discourse among theologians as well as scholars in the humanities. Post-structuralism problematized, and effectively undermined, the tacit confessionalism of these second-wave "political theologians," who often invoked non-traditional biblical, or Christian doctrinal, positions to advocate for their own distinctive versions of a radical or "emancipatory" politics.

By the early 1990s, however, a new kind of "secularized" as well as "globalized" strand of politico-theological thinking was starting to germinate within the post-structuralist framework of humanistic theory. This new template—what we can dub the "third wave"—relied heavily on classical Western political theory in ways that its predecessor had largely scanted. It was sparked by what came to be known as the "theological turn," or "religious turn," in European philosophy under the influence of the by-now dominant figure of Jacques Derrida. In Derrida's case, his religious turn coincided with a so-called "political turn," as was conspicuously evident in his *Specters of Marx* (1993) in which he redefined "deconstruction" as *justice* itself, while contextualizing it in terms of the "messianic."

This decisive theopolitical shift in Derrida's writings was concurrent with a revival in interest in Schmitt himself, who had been *de facto* blacklisted for over a generation by Western academics because of his collaboration with Nazism during the 1930s. Derrida first takes up Schmitt in a serious way in his *Politics of Friendship* (1994), focusing on the latter's famous rendering of the "concept of the political" with respect to the "friend/enemy distinction." Toward the end of that decade and throughout the few years prior

Foreword

to his death from pancreatic cancer in 2004, Derrida devoted most of his interest to Schmitt's concept of "sovereignty," as exemplified in his last two published works—*The Beast and the Sovereign* (2002) and *Rogues* (2003). *The Beast and the Sovereign*, consisting of unpublished seminar lectures, was not so much an exercise in political theology, per se, as a meditation on the singularity of the agential "I" and the full panoply of implications for Aristotle's definition of the human as both *zoon logikon* ("rational animal") and *zoon politikon* ("political animal"). But what gave Derrida's forays into the Schmittian expanse of sovereign decision-making—a venture for which he leveraged Rousseau to show that the logic of the latter could have democratic just as well as authoritarian outcomes—a measure of profound philosophical import was his refusal to rely on recognizable religious or moral assumptions.

Derrida effectively undertook a "deconstructive" reading of political theory that dissociated the formation of laws and states from Western metaphysics and what he all along had called "onto-theology." In his last lectures Derrida made the following observation: "If we must still speak of sovereignty . . . it will be another sovereignty," not one based on certain "constitutional" first principles of political accountability, but "one foreign to ontic power, and therefore foreign to political theology and to creationism, and to fundamentalism, in all senses of the term, in particular the sense that refers to a founding God."[3] In short, any political theology can no longer be construed as "theology" at all in the conventional sense of the word because it does not begin with the presuppositions of ecclesiastic consensus but with the conundrum of the political itself as the consequence of what in an earlier essay he called "force," which can only be understood as the "mystical foundation of authority."[4] Thus the question of what constitutes political theology as we transit into the fledgling decades of the third millennium is now up for grabs with ramifications that could

---

3. Derrida, *Beast and the Sovereign*, 215.

4. See Derrida, "Force of Law." I take up this analysis myself in Raschke, *Force of God*.

Foreword

not possibly have been foreseen by Schmitt and his successors during the century that went before.

In *Christian Political Theology in an Age of Discontent*, Jonathan Cole pulls few punches in laying out the kind of quandary in which the practitioners and advocates for the field find themselves these days. In his introduction, Cole reminds us forcefully that in the age of grandstanding politicians, Twitter mobs, fake news, and a routine overindulgence in social media to set what turn out to be incendiary, but ephemeral agendas, theological concerns often seem to be more substantive and "rational" than what passes for "politics" nowadays. The vast and rich complexity of the human condition as a whole, which political theory historically has sought to plumb as well as illuminate at the notional level, now requires a certain transcendental perspective which only the theological mind can supply.

But what kind of "theological" insight proves to be appropriate in this increasingly confused state of affairs? Unlike the variety of contemporary "secular" philosophers such as Derrida, Slavoj Žižek, and Alain Badiou, who have tried their hand in recent years at doing what is unmistakably political theology in the familiar sense of the word without falling back on any kind of traditional Christian symbologies or conceptual commitments, Cole wants to stake out a distinctive position that is neither *a-religious* nor blissfully *multi-religious*. The Christian point of view has both shaped and stamped for two millennia serious reflection on politics as we know it, chiefly because of the common Graeco-Roman semiotic milieu in which both theology and political thought has been seeded, grown, and thrived for the same extended time period. Broadly imagined, political theology has always been, and in a certain fashion *must always remain*, a peculiar type of hybrid disciplinary praxis that locates itself within the *teleology* of Greek *and* Christian thinking. "My approach to political theology," Cole writes,

> is shaped by the Greek insight that politics is both an art (*techne*) and science (*episteme*), which is to say that it is an activity with a telos, the accomplishment of which

requires practical skill, intellectual expertise, and wisdom. What I have sought to achieve in this collection of essays is to model a mode of theopolitical analysis that approaches political theology as both art and science in this Greek sense. This mode of theopolitical analysis seeks to mediate Scripture and theological doctrine in a way that meaningfully illuminates political reality, or aspects thereof.[5]

At first glance such a statement strikes us as fairly conventional, if not even orthodox, in its implications. But the issue of "political reality," Cole stresses, is a far more fraught and sprawling one than typical formulations of what we might term a *Christian politics*. Even if one surveys the lengthy and checkered record of Christian engagement with, as well as participation in, the political sphere, it becomes almost impossible to find a truly normative pattern of response. Protestant theologians in particular have frequently fallen back on the query of "What would Jesus do?" However, the practice of using Jesus as a prototype of political activism is egregiously flawed in its refusal to assess the actual social and historical conditions which contextualized his actions in that particular day and age, not to mention the enormous differences between the contemporary neoliberal world order and Roman-occupied Judea in the first century. "All too often one encounters a tendency," Cole argues "to reduce political theology to a handful of moral injunctions, such as "love thy neighbor," or biblio-theological concepts, such as covenant, as if either constituted a viable basis for organizing and running twenty-first-century economies in the midst of an epoch-making digital revolution and on the precipice of revolutions in artificial intelligence and bio-technology."[6]

Unfortunately, in popular and clerical settings, especially among many today who identify as proponents of the "Christian left," that is exactly what political theology seems to have become. And it also explains why political theology, Cole has quipped,

---

5. See Introduction of this book.
6. See Introduction of this book.

Foreword

needs to "grow up and become a real discipline."[7] What passes for "political theology" is often "strong in theology and weak in politics."[8] Whereas many of our most well-known gestures in this direction start from the theological and end up making judgements or observations about the political, Cole demands that we start from the ancient Greek idea of the *politeia* itself. Political theology itself must contrive "a foundational concept from which a definition of 'political' can be developed."[9] Of course, in a broad manner of speaking, that describes precisely what Schmitt sought to do. Whereas the second-wave theologians of a half century ago strove to elaborate a viable, action-oriented hermeneutic for their own religious and ethical stances, the trajectory of political theology in this new moment leans in the direction of understanding what binds people together in the "new polis" of the twenty-first century.

For Cole, the challenge of figuring out how human beings are appropriately bonded together is one of "governance," one which Michel Foucault identified in the 1970s as the key to deciphering the intricate "power" connections among those who participate in the political processes of the present era. It is the problem of governance that makes political theory and political theology "practical" to the extent that we must now test all models of legitimation within the ambit of how real people actually interpret as well as internalize these theories. Neoliberalism has fostered a deep-reaching and truly planetary legitimation crisis that has managed to eradicate prolifically and by subtle and often imperceptible means the long-standing mechanisms of social and cultural solidarity that underwrote the plausibility structures of political authority. Religious beliefs, validated and maintained through their respective historical constellations of theological oversight and magisterial administration, sufficed as the primary instruments for legitimating the political order.

---

7. Cole, "Political Theology Needs to Grow Up."
8. See chapter 1 of this book.
9. See chapter 2 of this book.

Foreword

"Political theology," therefore, as Schmitt rightly discerned, in the past functioned as the invisible infrastructure for underwriting the complex universe of day-to-day interpersonal allegiances and relationships. But the atomization and commodification of these relationships under triumphal global capitalism has changed the equation quite significantly. Any assumed homology between *homo politicus* and *homo oeconomicus* in this unprecedented environment can no longer be taken for granted. Perhaps we should surmise that in such an environment the issue of legitimation no longer is one of vertical authorization, as Schmitt presumed, but one of finding some means of *horizontal validation* among the ever fractious and contingent elements of a de-politicized global economic hegemony. Cole does not necessarily undertake such a daunting and monumental task. But he indirectly identifies it as what he calls the "Greek problem" for political theology. The Schmittian imperative was to find an appropriate language for correlating the sovereignty of God, in accordance with the ancient Hebraic prototype of "divine kingship," with the sovereignty of an earthly ruler.

As Cole stresses, the Greeks themselves did not comprehend the political imperative in this manner, even though Christianity "developed its own civilization replete with its own political thought and political norms."[10] At the same time, "we are much closer now to Greece than to Christendom, at least at the institutional level, and for most Christian citizens of Western polities this appears to be entirely unproblematic and unremarkable."[11] Thus Christians are often aiming to exploit non-Greek standards of transcendental normativity (e.g., the covenantal and ethical demands of Yahweh) in order to work out immanent conflicts of political organization and rational criteria of belonging and citizenship. This contradiction often presents an insurmountable *aporia*, of which those who claim the mantle of political theology tend to be but dimly aware.

It is for this reason that if political theology is somehow to "grow up," it must become more consciously political and less

10. See chapter 4 of this book.
11. See chapter 4 of this book.

Foreword

inclined to rely on its own *a priori* theological system of presuppositions. One touchstone to which a more sophisticated political-theological, or "theopolitical," endeavor could programmatically refer would be the thought of Thomas Hobbes, who can be considered not just the first modern political theorist, but also the epoch's first *political theologian*. That is not to say we must adopt the veneration for the state apparatus that Hobbes famously, or infamously, enshrines. But one takeaway available to us from Hobbes's approach is his contention that "God's sovereign power and rule are manifest in and realized through the natural laws that Hobbes says govern the political order."[12] Couched in classical terms, this kind of deference to Hobbes means that as political theologians we are invariably committed to the priority of "reason over revelation."

Furthermore, as Cole opines: "The more one reflects on the theopolitical logic of *Leviathan* the more one gains the impression that Hobbes's intent was not to expound a theologically-warranted polity so much as to relegate the role of theology to the very margins of politics."[13] Hobbes's overarching intent, however, was not, according to Cole, to secularize political theory and reestablish it somehow on the basis of the "sovereign" rationality of either an enlightened despot or an educated republican assembly. Hobbes's "motive appears to have been to banish what he regarded as theological superstition from the field of politics, not erase the Christian God from the scene altogether."[14] So the most pressing agenda we face today in what many declare is a secular, or post-theological, age is what are those current "superstitions" that ought to be banished, if the political and the religious once again are to mutually sustain and enable each other in a fashion that classical thought deemed salutary.

I myself would urge that the biggest superstition in circulation these days is the distinctly American conviction that its political leaders must somehow come across as residuary exemplars of moral virtue, especially if they are cultivating a base of religious

12. See chapter 6 of this book.
13. See chapter 6 of this book.
14. See chapter 6 of this book.

xvii

Foreword

supporters. For instance, it has been quite common since the election of 2016 for liberals to criticize evangelical Christianity for supporting the presidency of Donald Trump despite the latter's egregious character flaws and evidence in his personal life of serious moral shortcomings. Of course, in recent history evangelical Christians have cited this very yardstick to measure political performance. The frantic effort in the late 1990s to impeach President Bill Clinton simply because of his dalliances with a Washington intern automatically comes to mind. Without necessarily criticizing or exculpating the political behavior of evangelicals in either instance, Cole in three separate essays in the latter half of the book (chapters 7–9) goes to considerable length to show that in the history of both Christian and non-Christian political thought the question of moral character among leaders may be an abiding concern for the electorate, but it has preciously little to do with the more weighty matters of legitimacy and the exercise of sovereignty. To drive home this point Cole devotes a fair amount of space analyzing the importance of John Calvin for the confection of political theory over the past five hundred years:

> The sharp distinction Calvin draws between the heavenly kingdom of Christ and the earthly civil government, his belief that the primary purpose of government is to restrain and remedy human wickedness, and his understanding that sometimes God exercises his authority through oppression, leaves little room for the type of utopianism often on display in other parts of the Christian theopolitical tradition, not to mention a host of secular political philosophies.[15]

Thus Calvin may possibly be regarded as the genuine article in the development of a twenty-first century political theology *avant la lettre*. Although a consummate "theologian," Calvin did not let the latter preoccupation stand in the way of his penchant for trenchant, if not at times ruthless, dissection of contemporary politics. In fact, his insistence on what he called the *duplex cognitio Dei* ("double-sided knowledge of God"), in which an appreciation

15. See chapter 8 of this book.

for divine majesty and glory contrasted sharply with a loss of all sentimentality for human achievements, made his political analysis not merely sagacious, but prophetic. The great superstition of today, in which so many religious thinkers and various political pundits *manqué* uncritically participate, is that politics, in order to be authentic, must hinge for the most part on the mobilization of idealistic dreamers and the invocation of fantastical dreamscapes. The genuine theopolitical impulse, however, has always been to relativize what remains speculative and visionary for the sake of making room for what is eminently possible, at least within the "providential" ordering of human passions and even their most sordid affairs.

As Cole concludes, political theology must not be compromised by anything other than the agenda of clarifying the more intimate paradoxes and intricacies of the political as it has presented itself to us since the time of Socrates. It, therefore, in contrast with "theology" *tout court* is obligated to set its face against all our present-day enthusiasms gauged in conformance with "the impossible standard of an undefined ideal politics that is perpetually promised but yet to materialize."[16] That, in fact, is what renders the "impossibility" of the transcendental ordering of our chaotic political situation eminently *possible*.

CARL RASCHKE

---

16. See chapter 12 of this book.

Acknowledgements

I WOULD LIKE TO thank Carl Raschke for giving me the opportunity to write for *Political Theology Today* (now *The Political Theology Network*) and subsequently *The New Polis,* and for his encouragement and support throughout. I am grateful to the Centre for Public and Contextual Theology at Charles Sturt University for the generous publication assistance grant which helped this book see the light of day. The following mentors and intellectual companions have each contributed to my intellectual development, and hence directly or indirectly to the shape of the ideas found in this book: Wayne Hudson, Stephen Pickard, Andrew Cameron, Geoff Broughton, Scott Cowdell, Paul Henderson, Stephen Chavura, Simon Kennedy, Edward Morgan, and Christos Yannaras. I would further like to thank those readers who took the time to post comments in response to the original essays—these prompted fruitful refinements that have made their way into the content of this book. Finally, and by no means least of all, I would like to thank my wife Eva for her unfailing love, steadfast support, and nourishing encouragement over the past two decades.

Introduction

ANARCHIST POLITICAL PHILOSOPHER PIERRE-JOSEPH Proudhon memorably defined theology as "the science of the infinitely absurd."[1] Proudhon, who made this remark in 1840, was well ahead of his time. For it is only more recently, thanks in no small part to the latter-day high priests of atheism, that religion is now widely held to be responsible for all manner of political problems large and small. Yet if the follies of the twentieth-century's secular political ideologies are any guide, removing theology from politics is no panacea against absurdity. The reason that politics is so liable to absurdity, by atheist and theist alike, is the fact that it fundamentally transcends human capability. That is to say that the complex set of mutually interacting variables that characterize the political arena transcend the fallible human minds, finite human lives, and fallen human natures which are expected to master it. This variability presents a real challenge to political analysis. As Jack Hayward soberingly observed, "political scientists have the capacity to offer some hindsight, a little insight and almost no foresight."[2] Today even the elemental task of describing political reality is contested, particularly in the context of fake news, post-truth, and ideological fragmentation, whereby alternative political realities now vie for allegiance (or a following on social media).

Adding theology to political analysis does not resolve the challenge posed by the latter's complexity. Nor does it lift the veil

1. Proudhon, *What is Property?*
2. Hayward, "British Approaches to Politics," 34.

of mystery that obscures political destiny. If anything, theology simply compounds the difficulty of political analysis by adding its own complex set of variables to the equation. It also comes with its own set of internal disputes, as even a cursory glance at the literature of contemporary biblical studies reveals, not to mention the well-worn doctrinal and ecclesial differences that have divided Christians for centuries.

Still, political theology is no more an option for the Christian than political thought is an option for the thinking human being. For we all live within a political order and under some form of political authority, both of which materially affect our lives and elicit from us some kind of response, whether it be protest, acquiescence, or cooperation. We all form, whether consciously or passively, certain ideas about the nature, purpose, and legitimacy of the political order in which we live and those entrusted to preside over it. The Christian believer cannot help but understand that political order in the light of his or her theological convictions. While those convictions might appear absurd to the growing chorus of religion's despisers, they are what make politics intelligible and meaningful to the Christian, recalling that the atheist has no special inoculation against the transcendent mystery of politics and the tragic absurdity to which it is susceptible.

And yet many Christians, perhaps even a majority, do not bring their theological convictions to bear on their political context in any self-reflective, critical, or systematic manner. This dereliction of duty, if it can be characterized as such, has indeed led some Christians into the realm of political absurdity. In an age in which Western citizens of all credos risk being politicized to death, it is paramount that Christians develop a robust political theology that can help them navigate, individually and ecclesially, apologetically and constructively, the turbulent political waters of their times. A political theology fit for this task must be intellectually compelling, yet still feasible and efficacious. The present book seeks to contribute to the development of such a political theology. It comprises a series of essays originally published on *The Political Theology Network* and *The New Polis* between 2016 and 2018, which probe the

Introduction

nature, purpose, and content of Christian political theology. Each essay has been revised, in some cases extensively, and placed into a coherent order. Together, they constitute an exploration of the possibilities and challenges of Christian political theology in the current age of discontent.

What binds them is a common theopolitical method which stems from the conviction that political theology, whether biblical, doctrinal, ecclesial, or historical, must speak meaningfully to political reality. This is to say that political theology must offer a cogent account of political reality and a feasible roadmap to operating within that reality. All too often one encounters a tendency to reduce political theology to a handful of moral injunctions, such as "love thy neighbor," or biblio-theological concepts, such as covenant, as if either constituted a viable basis for organizing and running twenty-first-century economies in the midst of an epoch-making digital revolution and on the precipice of revolutions in artificial intelligence and bio-technology.

My approach to political theology is shaped by the Greek insight that politics is both an art (*techne*) and science (*episteme*), which is to say that it is an activity with a telos, the accomplishment of which requires practical skill, intellectual expertise, and wisdom. What I have sought to achieve in this collection of essays is to model a mode of theopolitical analysis that approaches political theology as both art and science in this Greek sense. This mode of theopolitical analysis seeks to mediate Scripture and theological doctrine in a way that meaningfully illuminates political reality, or aspects thereof. The extent to which this method succeeds, or can be deemed fruitful, I leave to the critical judgment of readers.

Political theology now boasts a prolific and proliferating literature. However, little binds this literature together in terms of method, scope, and content, apart from adoption of the term "political theology" by authors in disparate fields. This diversity, which is a charitable way of saying incoherence, is particularly evident when one brings into focus the polar ends of the spectrum of work now designated as "political theology." At one end stand devout Christian believers, searching for "true" political insights and guidance in the Bible, theological doctrine, and the life of the church. At the other end stand secular theorists for whom "political theology" appears to be something of a fashionable buzzword to be sprinkled like garnish upon writing that makes no discernable use of theology (traditionally construed), and which inclines towards a type of political gnosticism that is all but indecipherable to the uninitiated. One encounters any number of permutations between these two poles.

Definitions of political theology consequently abound—a reflection of and testament to the "field's" incoherence. The prudent course of action in this context is to simply stipulate one's definition of political theology and then march on with benign disregard for the disputatious nature of the term. If nothing else, this approach has the virtue of providing clarity around the definition of political theology that governs a particular work, if none other. To that end I propose to use the following definition of *Christian* political theology in the present work (other types of course exist but mercifully fall outside the scope of this work):

> Political theology is a mode of *political* analysis that proceeds from the conviction that politics (however defined) is embedded within a Christian ontology and shaped to some extent by a Christian historical teleology.

By "Christian ontology" I mean to denote an ontology that accepts the truth of orthodox Christian theological claims such *imago Dei*, the incarnation, the exaltation of Christ, a coming apocalypse, and so on.[3] By "Christian historical teleology" I mean to suggest the notion that God in some sense directs, shapes, or intervenes in history with a view to bringing it to some kind of purposeful and meaningful consummation. Historical teleology is meant to capture theological concepts such as divine sovereignty, providence, and the work of the Holy Spirit. Suffice to say, a Christian ontology and historical teleology can be expected to profoundly affect the way one understands and approaches the political realm

---

3. Raschke argues that political theology is "*not* a theology of the political" but an inquiry into the "ontological grounding" of the political. Raschke, *Force of God*, xii. Emphasis original.

(both practically and theoretically). Political thought that shows evidence of a Christian ontology and Christian historical teleology signals the existence of political theology.

This particular construal of political theology intentionally leaves "politics/political" and "theology" undefined in order to accommodate different understandings of their respective semantic fields. The definition can therefore fruitfully accommodate theological diversity, such as the Orthodox doctrine of *theosis* and the evangelical doctrine of substitutionary atonement, as well as diverse definitions of politics, whether restricted to the activity of governments alone, power relations more widely, or the entire gamut of social relations.[4] The purpose of this definition is to qualitatively distinguish political theology from other types of political thought, namely political science. In the absence of such a distinction, political theology becomes meaningless. In contrast to Christian political theology, political science proceeds from a naturalistic ontology and view of history which deems the authoritative sources of Christian ontology and teleology, namely the aforementioned Christian doctrines, to be irrelevant to an understanding of the natural phenomenon of politics. This is what functionally separates political theology from both secular political science and much contemporary political philosophy.

The essays which follow each prosecute an argument in relation to a particular theopolitical question. Their intended audience is wide and diverse: academic theologians, theological students, pastors, Christian political actors, and Christian citizens from all walks of life interested in the intersection of their faith and politics. The overarching objective of each essay is to inform, stimulate, and provoke—provoke in the sense of sparking critical thought, not in the sense of rhetorical artifice. It is my hope that readers who do not find each and every one of my discrete arguments compelling will nevertheless come away informed, stimulated, and provoked to their profit. I can ask for nothing more.

4. Papanikolaou has investigated the implications of the doctrine of *theosis* ("divine-human communion") for an Orthodox political theology in *The Mystical as Political*.

1

The Challenge for Christian Political Theology[1]

INTRODUCTION

CHRISTIAN POLITICAL THEOLOGY PRESENTS a rather confusing picture. A cacophony of voices offers conflicting accounts of what the Bible supposedly says about politics and what a normative Christian attitude towards politics is supposed to look like. Many of these accounts infer or perform eisegesis on scriptural warrants for any number of contemporary political ideologies, movements, parties, and agendas unknown to the original authors. Many contributors evidently lack any tangible political experience or expertise in the highly specialized areas of public policy characteristic of contemporary politics. Moreover, English-speaking political theologians[2] are almost exclusively preoccupied with Western

---

1. Originally published as "Christian Political Theology Needs to Grow up and Become a Real Discipline," *The Political Theology Network*. For a thoughtful critical engagement with the original essay, see Bacon, "Why Exactly Does Political Theology Need to Become a "Real Discipline.""

2. In reality, most "political theologians" are simply theologians who have at some point published on the topic of political theology. Few self-identify as "political theologians," per se, even when they have employed the term in their writing. I apply the term here and throughout heuristically to denote

liberal democracy with little thought for how their ideas might relate to Christians living in China, Iran, or Nigeria. And while most political theologies propose a normative ethic for Christian political engagement, they rarely, if ever, test these norms against case studies of actual regimes, past or present.

The confusion evident in Christian political theology is mirrored in the bewildering diversity of conflicting popular Christian attitudes towards politics. Christians find themselves on opposing sides of just about every major policy debate. There are Christians who earnestly believe God is self-evidently a liberal or progressive and others who just as earnestly believe he is self-evidently a conservative. In times past God has apparently been in favor of empire, hereditary monarchy, socialism, anarchism, and fascism. In the eyes of others God is utterly disinterested in politics. In the eyes of yet others he stands implacably opposed to the very idea of politics.

THE RATIONALE FOR POLITICAL THEOLOGY

Political theology is *unavoidable* and *indispensable* for the Christian and the church alike. It is unavoidable because Scripture invites reflection on politics, everyone lives under some form of political authority, and Christian churches occupy public space. Scripture invites (some might say demands) reflection on politics in several ways. Firstly, Scripture uses political concepts to convey theological truths. Political concepts such as "kingship," "judgment," "law," and "citizenship" are used in Scripture to articulate the relationship between God and his creation, especially his image-bearers. So key theological concepts, such as God's kingship, unavoidably have implications for how the Christian will view politics.

Secondly, Scripture provides a narrative of God's activities in human history. As a consequence, Scripture contains descriptions and interpretations of *actual* historical regimes and political developments, which have a greater or lesser bearing on how many

---

any thinker or scholar, theologian or otherwise, who has produced work that meets the definition of political theology stipulated in the introduction.

of the stories in the Bible are interpreted. The history of God's interaction with the world, irrespective of how it is interpreted, is inextricably intertwined with politics.

Thirdly, there are parts of Scripture that contain explicit exhortations in relation to what we might characterize today as politics. The most famous (and contentious) such passage is Rom 13:1: "Let every person be subject to the governing authorities; for there is no authority except from God, and those authorities that exist have been instituted by God."[3]

Reflection on politics is also unavoidable for the Christian because all humans live under some form of political authority that materially affects their lives, forcing them to think about politics and to make judgments about how they interact with political authorities. In fact, membership of a political order is involuntary—everybody is born under some form of political authority, even illegal aliens—and people can only remove themselves from a political order with great difficulty, if at all. So everybody, Christian and atheist alike, forms at least some opinions about politics and has at least some interaction with political authorities.

Political theology is further unavoidable for the fact that the church occupies public space. This is a product of two features of Jesus' ministry: it was public and spawned a social movement. If Jesus' ministry were not public, he would not have come to the attention of the religious and political authorities of his day. And if his ministry had not spawned a social movement, i.e., if he had not gathered followers who aided and participated in his ministry, then he likely would not have been deemed a threat by those same authorities. These two features of Jesus' ministry remain constitutive of the church. It is public and still functions like a social movement. As a consequence, churches unavoidably have a relationship with a political order and with the political authorities presiding over that order.

Political theology is indispensable for the Christian and the church today because traditional Christian beliefs and practices are increasingly matters of public controversy as cultural norms

3. All biblical quotes are taken from the NRSV.

and attitudes shift. In addition, the church's public role is no longer as secure as it once was in Western nations—Christian churches increasingly find themselves having to defend their public activities and even their very right to exist. This makes an apologetic and constructive political engagement imperative for Christians in the twenty-first century.

THE MISSING "POLITICAL" IN POLITICAL THEOLOGY

The fundamental problem with contemporary political theology, and a source of the confusion that characterizes theopolitical discourse, is that it is strong in theology and weak in politics. Given the importance of the concept of "politics" for the field of *political* theology, it is remarkable how infrequently this central term is defined in writings on the subject.[4] This is no trivial point. *Political* theology, after all, without the "political" is merely theology.

The failure to see the significance of defining "politics" in political theology is indicative of a broader disinterest in close examination of the phenomenon of politics by political theologians. There is much analysis of what the Bible purportedly does or doesn't say about politics, what the political significance is or isn't of the Christ-event, and what the existence of the church means for political authority, but often very little analysis of politics as a distinct phenomenon in its own right, i.e., its meaning, nature, and purpose in human social life and history. As a consequence, much political theology tends to say more about the Bible, theological doctrine, and the church than it does about politics.

It becomes clear on closer inspection that some of the fundamental points of difference in political theology trace their roots back to very different implicit conceptions of "politics" brought to the interpretation of the Bible, Christian doctrine, history, and tradition. This is one factor that gives political theology its sense

---

4. See the following chapter for more extensive discussion of this point.

The Challenge for Christian Political Theology

of incoherence, for it is often unclear if political theologians, when they address "politics," are actually talking about the same thing.

Part of the problem possibly stems from the fact that politics is nowhere defined in Scripture. The adjective "political," derived from the Greek term *polis* (city), does not occur in Scripture.[5] The terms "politics" and "political" thus do not appear in English translations of either the New or Old Testaments. It is perfectly understandable why the biblical authors saw no need to define politics. They were not writing treatises on political theory. It is, on the other hand, difficult to understand how someone engaged in *political* theology could see this as unimportant.

Moreover, politics is researched, analyzed, written about, and discussed at a volume, regularity, and degree of publicity that political theology simply is not. Given the phenomenon that political theologians and secular political thinkers analyze is *shared* and *observable,* there is much to be gained from a Christian theological engagement with secular political thought.[6] Such an engagement could potentially help political theologians find greater clarity around the constitutive concept of "political."

THE CHALLENGE OF POLITICAL PROFESSIONALIZATION AND EXPERTISE

A great challenge for political theology is the professionalization of contemporary politics, which has seen politics develop, for good or ill, into an arena of expertise. With few exceptions, contributors to theopolitical discourse appear to have spent their

---

5. Several derivatives of *polis* do occur, such as *politeuma*, translated as "citizenship" in Phil 3:20, and *politeia*, translated as "citizenship" in Acts 22:28 and "commonwealth" in Eph 2:12. The English terms "politics" and "political" do not occur in the NRSV translation of the Hebrew Bible. The Greek term *polis*, however, does occur with relative frequency in the Septuagint and the Greek New Testament. *Polis* had come to mean simply "city" in the first-century Jewish context, losing the richer tapestry of meaning it once possessed in its original Greek context.

6. See chapter 5 for my discussion of the relationship between Christian political theology and secular political philosophy.

careers in academia, the church, or a mixture of the two. This is not a criticism per se, for this is exactly where one might expect, or indeed wish, to find theologians. But in today's technocratic world where politics is the realm of professionals, whether in the form of elected representatives, advisors, civil servants, or journalists, analyzing politics from the sidelines can be an obstacle to understanding how politics functions in practice.

Much work in political theology fails to observe Roger Scruton's dictum that "the reality of politics is action."[7] As a consequence, theopolitical discourse can incline towards abstraction, seemingly unencumbered by considerations of whether the ideas discussed are feasible and implementable. In some cases, it is difficult to even discern whether a theopolitical proposal has any practical implications for political action at all.

Meanwhile, political decisions are inexorably made *daily*.[8] Just consider for a moment the criticism political leaders come under for perceived inaction, indecisiveness, or undue delay in decision-making. That is not to suggest that *thinking* about politics is unimportant. Scruton did not just say that politics is action; he also highlighted that *thought* governs action.[9] So the way we think about politics is inextricably linked to the way we act politically. Political theology is not wrong therefore to pay attention to how Christians ought to think about politics. It could however do a better job of relating Christian political thought to Christian political action.

There is, of course, no shortage of professional Christian politicians, advisors, officials, and journalists. But they are rarely professional theologians, and generally do not engage in theopolitical discourse, in spite of practicing the art of political theology

---

7. Scruton, *Meaning of Conservatism*, 1.

8. Finnis observes that "for most . . . co-ordination problems there are, in each case, two or more available, reasonable, and appropriate solutions, none of which, however, would amount to a solution unless adopted to the exclusion of the other solutions available, reasonable, and appropriate for that problem." Finnis, *Natural Law and Natural Rights*, 232.

9. Scruton, *Meaning of Conservatism*, 1.

The Challenge for Christian Political Theology

(consciously or unconsciously).[10] We have, therefore, on the one hand political theologians with little to no experience or expertise in the profession of politics, and, on the other hand, Christian political professionals with little to no theological training. There would be great mutual benefit in bringing these two worlds into deeper conversation and collaboration.

A related challenge for political theology is the sheer complexity and specialization of policy-development and implementation in modern nation-states. People spend whole careers developing expertise in specific areas of public policy through study, research, and professional experience. The political theologian, meanwhile, who has a host of non-political duties, obligations, and commitments, often lacks the opportunity and resources to develop substantive expertise in specific areas of public policy. Political theologians could address this gap by making the effort to better acquaint themselves with some areas of public policy. The political theologian, for example, could test their theories or proposed norms by studying a particular policy area in consultation with experts and political professionals with relevant experience.

POLITICAL THEOLOGY'S SURPRISING DISREGARD FOR POLITICAL HISTORY

Another weakness hampering political theology is its surprising lack of interest in political history. If political theologians take account of political history at all, they generally do so with a parochial focus on the history of Israel, the first-century Greco-Roman world, Christendom (Byzantine political history and political thought is largely ignored in Protestant political theology[11]), the Enlightenment, and liberal democracy. Other historical regimes and civilizations are generally ignored or treated superficially. The

---

10. See the following chapter for my discussion of political theology as an "art."

11. Contemporary Orthodox political theology has only recently begun to flower, redressing the long Western (in the theological sense) bias of the field. See, for example, Stoeckl et al., *Political Theologies in Orthodox Christianity*.

significance of this historical matrix needs no justification for the political theologian writing in English, as it articulates the genealogy of their political context. But is it really a sufficiently deep and broad basis upon which to draw normative conclusions about politics given its universal character?

Political history begins well before the emergence of Israel. At the dawn of recorded history in the fourth millennium BC, both Egypt and Sumer already evince well-established and complex political orders. Systematic empirical and theoretical analysis of politics begins in fifth-century Greece.[12] Moreover, Christian reflection on politics is not the only species of political theology. There are parallel Jewish and Islamic traditions of theological reflection on politics which continue unabated to this day.

The point is not that Christian political theology has some sort of obligation to look outside its own history and Scripture for its political concepts and norms. It is to suggest, rather, that Christian political theology could establish a more intellectually rigorous foundation if it were to broaden its horizon to include the political history of regimes and peoples that fall outside the scope of sacred history.

THE PROBLEM OF CRITICAL MASS

A final challenge for political theology is the lack of critical mass in scholarship on the topic. Political theology is still a relatively marginal sub-discipline of theology and hardly a staple on the syllabus of the average theology school or seminary, although interest in the topic appears to be growing.[13]

Recognizing that political theology is in many respects still in its infancy as a discipline can help us to place existing contributions into context.[14] Key contributions to the field, dating back to

---

12. See chapter 4 for my discussion of the relationship between Greek political thought and Christian political theology.

13. O'Donovan has described political theology as a "pseudo-disciplinary designation." O'Donovan, *Ways of Judgment*, ix.

14. Lloyd and True, in outlining their vision for the journal *Political*

the 1970s, deserve to be regarded as pioneering works.[15] They are the firstfruits of theologians who beat a path from the comfortable confines of theology into the dense, wild jungle of politics. We therefore owe a debt of gratitude to the likes of John Howard Yoder (Mennonite), Reinhold Niebuhr (Reformed), Oliver O'Donovan (Anglican), Johann B. Metz (Catholic), and Christos Yannaras (Orthodox), to name but a few, for beating the path along which subsequent generations (including this author) tread. But the time has come to pave the paths trodden by these pioneers to enable high-volume traffic and trade to proceed.

CONCLUSION

Given Scripture and the nature of the church demand some level of thought about politics, and given the fact that we all inescapably have to interact to some degree with a political order, the choice confronting the Christian is not that between *a* political theology or *no* political theology. Rather, it is between a *good* political theology or a *bad* political theology. Good political theology requires deeper reflection on politics as an observable phenomenon in its own right. It also requires deeper engagement with secular political thought and political history, as well as with the practical art of politics. That is achievable. But it requires political theology to mature into a bona fide discipline. Such a transition depends on a greater number of aspiring or established theologians choosing political theology as a vocation, and then dedicating themselves to the long study of politics required to develop true expertise in the field (while at the same time gaining some mastery over the vast and complex tradition of theological thought itself). In turn,

---

Theology, note that "political theology is an emerging field." Their vision seeks to address some of the criticisms raised here, such as the narrow Western focus of much contemporary Christian political theology, by including global voices from Africa, Asia, and India, as well as Islam. Lloyd and True, "What Political Theology Could Be," 506.

15. I take up the issue of political theology's contemporary origins in chapter 3.

this requires theology schools and seminaries to invest greater resources in political theology in recognition that it ought to be regarded as an essential component of a contemporary theological education that aims to aid the church as it contends with a rapidly developing political context.

2

The Art of Political Theology[1]

WHAT IS POLITICAL THEOLOGY? That is the question invariably put to the self-professed political theologian by Christian and non-Christian alike. It is a difficult question to answer, in part because of the proliferation of definitions advanced in scholarship. Inquirers do not wish to be given a menagerie of definitions, particularly arcane academic definitions. Pointing out that the definition is "contested" and difficult to define just seems to confirm people's worst prejudices about out-of-touch ivory towers. In the previous chapter I suggested that one of the weaknesses of contemporary Christian political theology is its failure to properly and clearly define the constitutive concept "political." In what follows I survey several definitions of political theology in an effort to substantiate this claim. I will then suggest that political theology is perhaps best conceived as an "art." I close by offering my own definition of the *art* of political theology.

I begin with Cavanaugh and Scott's "expansive" definition in the *Blackwell Companion to Political Theology*:

---

1. Originally published as "The Art of Political Theology—Finding the Right Definition and the Proper Set of Questions," *The Political Theology Network*.

> Political theology is, then, the analysis and criticism of political arrangements (including cultural-psychological, social, and economic aspects) from the perspective of differing interpretations of God's ways with the world.[2]

The problem in relation to this definition revolves around the opacity of the term "political arrangements." Its linkage to the categories "cultural-psychological," "social," and "economic" clearly envisages a rather broad scope, even if restricted to "aspects" thereof. In this context "political" appears to relate to the entire gamut of human experience. The scope of "political arrangements" is subsequently qualified by the clarification that "the political is broadly understood as the use of structural power to organize a society or community of people."[3] Even so, "political," as it functions in the concept "political theology," lacks clarity.

Hent de Vries's definition in *Political Theologies: Public Religions in a Post-Secular World* provides a more complex, and consequently more abstruse, definition:

> The concept of "political theology" connotes ... the "ever-changing relationships between political community and religious order, in short, between power [or authority: *Herrschaft*] and salvation [*Heil*]." Yet its contemporary range and implications reach further and encroach upon the central questions of political philosophy and political theory, in its comparative anthropological, sociological, economic, and juridical varieties, from which its original metaphysical impetus must also be distinguished. In addition to theorizing "the political," "political theology" also enters into relationship with urgent questions of daily "politics," without, of course, being immediately (or fully) rendered (or contradicted) by them.[4]

Here we have the concepts "political community," "religious order," "power," "political philosophy," "juridical varieties," and

---

2. Cavanaugh and Scott, *Blackwell Companion to Political Theology*, 1.
3. Cavanaugh and Scott, *Blackwell Companion to Political Theology*, 1.
4. de Vries, "Introduction," 25. This particular definition is introduced as systematic and traditional.

"metaphysical impetus." We also have the activities: "encroaching upon," "theorizing," and "entering into relationship." Is there a definition of "political" here? The closest de Vries comes to defining "political" is to ostensibly equate it with "power," itself a rather broad category in the absence of further qualification.

Hovey and Phillips offer a more succinct definition in *The Cambridge Companion to Political Theology*:

> An inquiry carried out by Christian theologians in relation to the political, where the political is defined broadly to include the various ways in which humans order common life.[5]

Unlike de Vries and Cavanaugh and Scott, Hovey and Phillips appear to restrict "political theology" to the rarefied circles of professional theologians. But like de Vries and Cavanaugh and Scott, they connect political theology to a broad, albeit ill-defined, conception of the "political": "The various ways in which humans order common life."

Not all definitions are so open-ended. Wolterstorff defines "political theology" in *The Mighty and the Almighty* as follows:

> Political theology is not theology with a political cast; it is theology of or about the political, more specifically, theology of or about the state.[6]

The virtue of Wolterstorff's definition is that it draws a more restrictive, and hence more manageable, scope around the notion of "political." But is it enough to simply equate the "political" with the "state?" Is there a Palestinian or Kurdish politics? What about the UN? What about a transnational organization like ISIS? And what of political communities that predate the emergence of the nation-state? Moreover, the state, like most political concepts these days, is contested and itself difficult to define.[7] So without further elabo-

---

5. Hovey and Phillips, *Cambridge Companion to Political Theology*, xi–xii.
6. Wolterstorff, *Mighty and the Almighty*, 2 (footnote 3).
7. Hay, for example, notes that "no concept is more central to political discourse and political sociology than that of the state. Yet the concept remains elusive and, for some at least, illusory; the term being notoriously difficult to

ration or qualification, identifying the "political" with the "state" might prove too restrictive and at the same time unclear.

A different type of definition is offered by Oliver O'Donovan in *The Desire of the Nations*:

> The name "political theology" is generally given to proposals . . . which draw out an earthly political discourse from the political language of religious discourse.[8]

The religious discourse O'Donovan has in mind is the Bible and its interpretation and application by the church throughout history. But this definition still leaves open the question of what precisely the "political" in "political discourse" denotes, other than that the "political" and "theological" are interwoven: "Theology is political simply by responding to the dynamics of its own proper themes."[9]

O'Donovan did eventually provide a definition of "political" in *The Ways of Judgment*, the companion he wrote to *The Desire of the Nations* nine years later. That definition is "activities with a direct relation to government, but not only those with a direct relation to elected office."[10] Like Wolterstorff, O'Donovan's definition has the virtue of being restrictive. In fact, it is narrower and clearer than Wolterstorff's "state." Yet it still suffers from the problem identified with Wolterstorff's definition above, to the extent that it appears to leave no room for political communities without a government, at least conventionally defined, unless we are prepared to speak of ISIS and the UN as governments.

In spite of their obvious differences, these definitions all share a common characteristic: deficient conceptions of "political" for the purposes of providing lucid definitions of "political theology." It is true that they can be sorted according to a spectrum running from more expansive to more restrictive conceptualizations of the "political," but in each case "political" remains ill-defined.[11]

---

define." Hay, "Neither Real Nor Fictitious," 459.

8. O'Donovan, *Desire of the Nations*, 2.
9. O'Donovan, *Desire of the Nations*, 3.
10. O'Donovan, *Ways of Judgment*, 56.
11. I note that this criticism arguably does not apply to O'Donovan's

This is not to say that the definitions are erroneous. None makes a category mistake, such as suggesting that "political theology" investigates the mating habits of stick insects. Few would demur that "politics," however conceived, does legitimately involve discussion of "states," "governments," "power," and aspects of "social," "economic," and "cultural" activity. But what does it say about political theology that one of its constitutive concepts, namely "political," is routinely defined in such a way that makes the "emerging field" incoherent, at least with respect to its purview?

It is worth highlighting two additional factors that compound the prevailing confusion around the term "political theology." Firstly, there are disciplines on either side of political theology that intersect with it and plough common terrain. On the *political* side of the equation is political philosophy and political science. On the *theology* side is public theology.[12] On both sides there is (political) ethics, Christian and secular. The precise differences and interrelationships between these disciplines are far from clear. Still, scholars generally identify with one rather than one of the others (there are exceptions of course), indicating that there is at least some functional difference between them.

Exacerbating the confusion is the fact that in spite of political theology only emerging in the late 1960s as a concept in English-language theology, theopolitical thinking has never really been absent from Christian theology.[13] Many regard Augustine's *City of God* as the first great work in political theology, or at least the first work containing something that could be described as a

---

definition given in *The Ways of Judgment*, although the absence of a definition in *The Desire of the Nations* is indicative of my contention that the term is all-too-often left undefined in self-professed works in political theology.

12. Defined by Day and Kim as "the church reflectively engaging with those within and outside its institutions on issues of common interest and for the common good." Day and Kim, *A Companion to Public Theology*, 2. I also note that "theology" comes with its own definitional difficulties and one could similarly argue that this constitutive term is not sufficiently well-defined in some or all of the examples provided.

13. See the next chapter for more detailed discussion of the complex history of the term "political theology."

political theology.¹⁴ Yet many definitions of "political theology" inadvertently make politics a modern phenomenon rather than the ancient phenomenon it undoubtedly is. Still, one should bear in mind Karl Popper's wise aphorism that "one should never try to be more precise than the problem situation demands."¹⁵ To that end, it is important to recognize that politics is a complex phenomenon that demands a complex definition. The complexity of the term "political" is brought to, rather than caused by, political theology. Perhaps, then, we should not be so perturbed by definitional pluralism. The problem, as I see it, is not so much the lack of consensus about how to define the term "political theology" so much as the frequent failure to provide clarity around what is denoted by the constitutive concept "political" in particular works professing to be in, or on, something called "political theology." This lack of clarity frustrates critical theopolitical discourse.

It is also important to keep in mind that political theology is not the exclusive preserve of academia. All Christians unavoidably do some thinking about the intersection of faith and politics, even if it is just to turn their backs on the latter. More importantly, Christians who venture into politics as a vocation do not have the same luxury of celebrating theoretical diversity as scholars do. By necessity they must come to concrete judgments on specific political, policy, and even philosophical questions, and be willing to see those judgments implemented.

This is why I propose to conceive political theology as an "art." By art I mean "skilled execution or agency," or "a method of doing a thing."¹⁶ Art is designed to capture both the theoretical and practical elements of political theology, and as I indicated in the introduction to this book, this view of politics has an ancient pedigree. This brings us to the question of how I propose to define political theology. Given my criticism of the opacity of "political"

---

14. Phillips, *Political Theology*, 23. Some go back further still to the *Epistle to Diognetus*, likely written between 117 and 313. Holmes, "Introduction," 689.

15. Popper, *Unended Quest*, 24.

16. *Macquarie Complete Australian Dictionary*, "art."

in the definitions examined earlier, I begin with a discussion of the concept "political."

There is a propensity to define politics very broadly. Kenneth Shepsle, by way of example, defines "politics" in *Analyzing Politics: Rationality, Behavior, and Institutions* as "utterly indistinguishable from the phenomena of group life generally."[17] This definition appears to negate the very possibility of treating "politics" as a distinct phenomenon, a somewhat counter-intuitive conclusion for a book called *Analyzing Politics*. If politics is to be a meaningful category at all, it must be capable of distinction. It must, in other words, work from the premise that there are both political and non-political activities in human life, and then define that distinction in some manner.

I believe what is called for is a foundational concept from which a definition of "political" can be developed. I propose "governance," which I construe as "the institutions, rules, and administration of authority" (this is a modification of the entry for "government" found in the *Oxford Concise Dictionary of Politics*[18]). The virtue of anchoring a definition of "political" in "governance" is that it makes the foundation of our definition something concrete and tangible, i.e., something that can be described empirically.

Governance, moreover, has the flexibility to accommodate the breadth and depth of diverse "political arrangements" past and present. Democracies, dictatorships, and everything in between have institutions, rules, and mechanisms for administering authority. Governance can also be identified and described in the multiplicity of political arrangements of the past, whether the Athenian democracy of Pericles, the Abbasid Caliphate of Harun al-Rashid, or the Iroquois League in North America. Governance can also be observed in non-state entities like the UN and even ISIS.

With this foundation set, the question then becomes how far to extend the notion of governance, or rather how far beyond governance to stretch the notion "political"? As O'Donovan astutely observes in *The Ways of Judgment*, even a poem, in the

---

17. Shepsle, *Analyzing Politics*, 11.
18. McLean and McMillan, "Government."

right context, can be political.[19] I propose to define "political" as both the activities undertaken *by* governing institutions and those undertaken by the governed *in relation to* governing institutions. Thus, any activity that responds to, seeks to influence, or mobilize support for or against some aspect of governance, including decisions or activities of any governing institution, can rightly be regarded as "political."

This recognizes that almost any aspect of human life has the *potential* to be political, but that it is context that *actually* determines whether this is the case or not. For example, a musician is not "political" merely by virtue of being a musician. There is nothing intrinsically political about music. However, should a musician perform at a protest which "seeks to influence or mobilize support for or against an aspect of governance," then the act of playing their music in that context, irrespective of the content of the lyrics, can be deemed "political."

With this conception of "political" in mind it is possible to proceed to a definition of *political* theology. The definition that seems to commend itself in light of the foundation I have set is simply "a theology of governance." But this still feels too narrow, particularly in light of my proposal to conceive political theology as an art. I therefore propose to define political theology as "asking theological questions related to governance *and* then acting upon the answers to such questions." There is no limit to the type of theological questions that can be asked in this context. Nor should there be. Indeed, the questions will necessarily vary according to political context. The types of questions I have in mind range from exegetical questions, such as, "what does Scripture say about governance?" to historical questions such as "what was the early church's attitude to governance?" They range from traditional theological questions such as, "what is the role of providence in governance?" to ecclesiological questions, such as, "what is the proper relationship of the church to secular governance?" They also include ethical questions, such as, "is it appropriate for a Christian to join a political party and run for office?"

19. O'Donovan, *Ways of Judgment*, 55.

In the introduction to this book I provided a definition of political theology centered on ontology and historical teleology. That definition aimed to differentiate Christian political theology from other modes of political thought. My definition deliberately left "political" and "theology" undefined in order to take account of the diverse ways in which political theology's constituent terms are defined across multiple traditions and political contexts. The ambition in providing that introductory definition was to establish that political theology is an area of intellectual inquiry that is meaningfully distinct. Here I have suggested that political theology can be thought of, and practiced, as an art. Accordingly, I have offered a normative definition of political theology as an art—one in which the constitutive term "political" is given more precise and circumscribed meaning than is often the case, while still leaving "theology" open in order to accommodate the diversity that is characteristic of contemporary theology. My proposal to treat political theology as an art is not meant to undermine my earlier definition of political theology as a *distinct* mode of political thought. It is simply to recognize that political theology is both an abstract area of intellectual inquiry *and* a practical activity requiring both skill and knowledge.

3

Carl Schmitt and the True German Origins of Christian Political Theology[1]

INTRODUCTION

"SOVEREIGN IS HE WHO decides on the exception."[2] Thus opens the book that is said to have given birth to political theology—Carl Schmitt's *Political Theology*, published in German in 1922.[3] This deceptively simple proposition opens a highly stimulating and

---

1. Originally published as "Carl Schmitt and the True German Origins of Political Theology," *The New Polis*.
2. Schmitt, *Political Theology*, 5.
3. The term "political theology" has a history predating Schmitt. Mikhail Bakunin used the term in French in a text called "The Political Theology of Mazzini," published in 1871. That text was a polemic against Giuseppe Mazzini and the term, which only appears in the title, was intended as a term of opprobrium towards Mazzini's theistic idealism (Bakunin, "Political Theology of Mazzini," 214). Interestingly, Burke used "political theologians" as a term of opprobrium in *Reflections on the Revolution in France*, 12 (published in 1790). Herrero traces the origin of the term back to the seventeenth century, with Simon van Heenvliedt's book *Theologico-Politica Dissertatio*, published in 1662, possibly representing that era's first usage of the term and followed in 1670 by Spinoza's *Tractatus Theologico-Politicus* (Herrero, "Carl Schmitt's Political Theology," 23). De Vries locates the first historical appearance of the term in the writings of Varro (116–27 BC) (De Vries, "Introduction," 25).

insightful examination of the relationship between sovereignty, law, and the state. But what does *Political Theology* have to do with "political theology" as that term is understood and used today? Very little as it turns out. In fact, Schmitt, as I argue below, appears to have played little role in the emergence of political theology in English-language scholarship.

The discussion proceeds in two parts: an examination of the content of the term "political theology" as it appears in the book of the same name, followed by an examination of the circumstances in which "political theology" emerged as an explicit concept in English-language scholarship.

SCHMITT'S USE OF THE TERM "POLITICAL THEOLOGY"

The first observation to make about *Political Theology* is that, title notwithstanding, it is not about "political theology" as that term is commonly understood today. *Political Theology* directly addresses the issue of "political theology" in only one of the four essays that comprise the book. Moreover, that chapter—aptly titled "Political Theology"—contains just three explicit references to the term, which happen to be the book's only references (I discuss an exception below). The titles of the remaining three essays paint a more accurate picture of the book's central concern: "Definition of Sovereignty," "The Problem of Sovereignty as the Problem of the Legal Form and of the Decision," and "On the Counterrevolutionary Philosophy of the State (de Maistre, Bonald, Donoso Cortés)."

It is telling that in their foreword and introduction to the book respectively, neither Tracy Strong nor George Schwab saw any particular need to discuss the concept of political theology. Strong explains that *Political Theology* is about the nature and prerogative of sovereign political authority in the West (with due regard for the role played by Western Christianity in its development).[4] Schwab describes the import of *Political Theology* as resting in its

---

4. Strong's foreword to Schmitt, *Political Theology*, vii.

contribution to "a deeper understanding of the political and constitutional history of the Weimar period," the insight it provides into "Schmitt's understanding of state, sovereignty, and politics," and its ongoing relevance "to our understanding of the functioning of the sovereign state."[5]

Thus, I ask again: what does *Political Theology* have to do with "political theology"? The fundamental argument advanced in the chapter called "Political Theology" is that "all significant concepts of the modern theory of the state are secularized theological concepts."[6] This is the idea most oft-cited in support of the claim that Schmitt was the progenitor of political theology. Schmitt argued that the "omnipotent God" came to replace the "omnipotent lawgiver" in the theory of the state, and that "the exception in jurisprudence [was] analogous to the miracle in theology."[7] As he explained,

> whoever takes the trouble of examining the public law literature of positive jurisprudence for its basic concepts and arguments will see that the state intervenes everywhere. At times it does so as a *deus ex machina*, to decide according to positive statute a controversy that the independent act of juristic perception failed to bring to a generally plausible solution; at other times it does so as the graceful and merciful lord who proves by pardons and amnesties his supremacy over his own laws.[8]

Schmitt's proposition about the secularization of theological concepts is fundamentally a historical argument. The nineteenth century saw God "radically pushed aside" such that legal authority and legitimacy became "identified with the lawfulness of nature, which applies without exception."[9] This contrasted with a mode of conservative counterrevolutionary political thought which

---

5. Schwab's introduction to Schmitt, *Political Theology*, xli.
6. Schmitt, *Political Theology*, 36.
7. Schmitt, *Political Theology*, 36.
8. Schmitt, *Political Theology*, 38.
9. Schmitt, *Political Theology*, 48.

supported "the personal sovereignty of the monarch" by using "analogies from a theistic theology."[10]

In conservative (mainly Catholic) theory of the state, the monarch was identified with God and occupied a position "exactly analogous to that attributed to God in the Cartesian system of the world."[11] Schmitt's key insight (credited to Kelsen and Leibniz before him[12]) is that there is a "systematic analogy between theological and juristic concepts" in spite of "the elimination of all theistic and transcendental conceptions and the formation of a new concept of legitimacy."[13]

But again, what does this have to do with political theology? At just three explicit references and a book title, it is actually difficult to say. In all three instances where the term "political theology" is used by Schmitt, it appears to denote a conservative theory of state propounded by writers supportive of the Restoration in the nineteenth century—the Cartesian defense of monarchy mentioned above. In one instance, Schmitt contrasts the "political theology" of the Restoration with "the radicals who opposed all existing order" and thus "directed . . . their ideological efforts against the belief in God altogether."[14] Another draws a parallel with contemporary (1920s) democratic thinking—the "pragmatic belief" in America "that the voice of the people is the voice of God," and Tocqueville's observation that "in democratic thought the people hover above the entire political life of the state, just as God does above the world."[15]

The three explicit references to "political theology" suggest that Schmitt applied the term in a rather specific and limited manner, namely, to denote a nineteenth-century German current of political thought about the state that had been superseded by Schmitt's day. But that would seemingly make the book's title

10. Schmitt, *Political Theology*, 37.
11. Schmitt, *Political Theology*, 46.
12. Schmitt, *Political Theology*, 37, 40.
13. Schmitt, *Political Theology*, 42, 51.
14. Schmitt, *Political Theology*, 50.
15. Schmitt, *Political Theology*, 49.

something of an eccentric choice. A clue to the puzzle of the title can be found in Schmitt's preface to the second edition in 1934, where he uses the term "political theology" (the aforementioned exception) in a rather different sense, as a heuristic for analyzing political theories and ideologies more generally.

There is a somewhat cryptic reference to "the thought processes of political theology," for instance, and a suggestion that the "idea" of political theology might be applicable to the notion of representation from the fifteenth century on, monarchy in the seventeenth century, the notion of neutral power in the nineteenth century, and even the modern administrative state.[16] It is possible Schmitt regarded the entire book as "political theology" in a methodological or theoretical sense.[17] In any event, Schmitt's use of the term "political theology" remains rather opaque.

THE TRUE GERMAN ORIGINS OF POLITICAL THEOLOGY

The origins of political theology are indeed German. It is just that Schmitt does not appear to be the German responsible. The first explicit and substantive discussion of "political theology" in English comes by way of German Catholic theologian Johann Metz, who in 1968—a full 46 years after Schmitt's *Political Theology*—published an essay in *The Harvard Theological Review* called "Religion and Society in the Light of a Political Theology"[18] (he also

16. Schmitt, preface to the second edition of *Political Theology*, 1.

17. According to Herrero, Schmitt used the concept "political theology" to denote a "theoretical field useful for understanding early modern historical and political phenomena." Herrero, "Carl Schmitt's Political Theology," 24.

18. Louis Midgley actually used the term in a sense akin to that used by Metz one year prior in his article "Ultimate Concern and Politics: A Critical Examination of Paul Tillich's Political Theology," in which he argued that "the basic categories of [Tillich's] philosophical theology constitute an elaborate and sophisticated political theology" (31). Metz, however, as far as I can ascertain, is the first Christian theologian to offer something (in English) self-described as a "political theology" in the normative sense under examination in the present book. Midgley, who is a Mormon scholar, merely used the term to describe the character of Tillich's political thought. It is noteworthy that the

discussed "political theology" in his book *Theology of the World*, published in English translation in 1969).

Unlike Schmitt's treatment of "political theology" as a heuristic for interpreting certain historical political theories, or as a means of designating a particular current of political thought in nineteenth-century Germany, Metz approached political theology as a "task" to be performed by theologians.[19] Metz envisaged "political theology" as both a "critical correction" to the "extreme privatizing tendency" of Christianity and "a positive attempt to formulate the eschatological message under the condition of our present society."[20]

This critical task entailed Christian theology "uncover[ing] the socio-political implications of its ideas and notions," a need arising from the breakdown of the erstwhile unity between religion and society.[21] Metz's overarching concern was to combat the privatization, and concomitant depoliticization, of Christianity. In *Theology of the World*, he would argue that "the deprivatizing of theology is the primary critical task of political theology."[22]

The positive task of political theology, according to Metz, entailed what he described as a post-critical "second reflection" on the relationship between religion and society.[23] Underpinning Metz's conception of political theology's constructive task was the conviction that salvation is public: "Christian salvation is intrinsically concerned with the world, not in a natural-cosmological sense, but in a socio-political sense . . . as a critically liberating force of this social world and its historical process."[24]

---

term "public theology" was apparently coined in 1974 (by Martin Marty), thus making its emergence contemporaneous with that of political theology. Day and Kim, *A Companion to Public Theology*, 3.

19. Metz, "Religion and Society," 507.
20. Metz, "Religion and Society," 507.
21. Metz, "Religion and Society," 508.
22. Metz, *Theology of the World*, 110.
23. Metz, "Religion and Society," 511.
24. Metz, "Religion and Society," 513. This idea was taken up by liberation theology. See, for example, Gutiérrez, *A Theology of Liberation*.

Metz's introduction of the term "political theology" to English-language theology was shortly thereafter followed by another German, Reformed theologian Jürgen Moltmann. In 1971, he penned an essay called "Political Theology" published in *Theology Today*.[25] Like Metz, Moltmann was preoccupied by the Enlightenment's relativization and privatization of Christian tradition and faith. He too approached political theology as a task—"Engag[ing] in a social, political, and psychological criticism of the Enlightenment in order to achieve a new state of consciousness."[26] The new state of consciousness he had in mind was a theological consciousness: "political theology is therefore not simply political ethics but reaches further by asking about the political consciousness of theology itself."[27] Moltmann set a christological foundation for political theology, on the basis that "the cross of Christ is . . . the one truly political point in the story of Jesus."[28]

Another German soon followed in the form of Dorothee Soelle, whose 1971 book *Political Theology* was translated into English in 1974 (the German title was *Political Theology: A Conversation with Rudolf Bultmann*). Though approaching political theology from a somewhat different perspective to that of Metz and Moltmann, she too nevertheless understood political theology to be a "program" that sought to "bring faith and action together more satisfactorily."[29] English-speaking theologians quickly embraced the concept of "political theology" and the term has occupied a place in the English theological lexicon ever since.

English-speaking theologians of the 1970s, however, were patently aware that the term "political theology" was of very recent provenance in their context. Alistair Kee, for example, in his preface to a 1974 volume he edited called *A Reader in Political*

---

25. Moltmann, "Political Theology."

26. Moltmann, "Political Theology," 7. Herrero describes Moltmann's approach to political theology as "affirmative political theology," in contrast to Schmitt's methodological usage of the concept (Herrero, "Carl Schmitt's Political Theology," 36).

27. Moltmann, "Political Theology," 8.

28. Moltmann, "Political Theology," 15.

29. Soelle, *Political Theology*, 2.

Theology, explained to readers that the "phrase" political theology had "only appeared in the last few years."[30] Interestingly, Migliore could already speak of "political theologians" as early as 1969.[31] The fact that the term "political theology" only began to gain currency amongst English-speaking theologians from the late 1960s might help to explain the oddity that one of that decade's most influential contributions to the discussion makes no mention at all of "political theology"—John Howard Yoder's *The Politics of Jesus* (published in 1972).[32] *The Politics of Jesus* is a timely reminder that politics was, and in fact had long been, an area of keen theological reflection in the English-speaking world at the moment German theology apparently bequeathed it the term "political theology."[33] Yoder too was motivated by frustration at the depoliticized private faith that then passed for Christianity. But Yoder and his ilk were addressing something then known as "social ethics," a term which appears to have been eventually supplanted by political theology.

Earlier references to the term "political theology" in English-language scholarship are infrequent and descriptive, such as Julian Obermann's 1935 essay called "Political Theology in Early Islam: Ḥasan Al-Baṣrī's Treatise on Qadar"[34] and Ernst Harwig Kantorowicz's 1957 book called *The King's Two Bodies: A Study*

---

30. Kee, *A Reader in Political Theology*, ix.

31. Migliore, "Biblical Eschatology and Political Hermeneutics," 116: "Among the new political theologians, especially Jürgen Moltmann . . . " Interestingly, Migliore indicates that, at the time of writing, "a number of theologians [were] currently at work on what is variously called 'political theology,' 'theology of social change,' and 'theology of revolution.'"

32. Discussed in more detail in chapter 10.

33. One can also point to earlier works that clearly fall within the scope of "political theology," but were not described as such in their day. See, for example, Micklem, *The Theology of Politics*, published in 1941, which contains a collection of essays "survey[ing] the intermediate country between theology and politics," on the premise that "our political philosophy, explicitly or implicitly, rests upon our theology" (x). One could also point to the oeuvre of Reinhold Niebuhr, probably America's most influential "political theologian" (applying the term retrospectively).

34. Obermann, "Political Theology in Early Islam."

in *Mediaeval Political Theology*.³⁵ Neither uses the term "political theology" in the sense meant by Metz, Moltmann, and Soelle.³⁶

WHITHER SCHMITT?

It appears that German theologians introduced the concept of "political theology" to English-speaking theologians in the late 1960s and early 1970s. However, precisely what influence Schmitt did or did not have on those German theologians is far from clear. A direct influence appears unlikely. Firstly, Metz, Moltmann, and Soelle simply make no reference to Schmitt. John Shelley, in the introduction to his translation of Soelle's *Political Theology*, notes *en passant* in a footnote that Schmitt and Erik Peterson engaged in a debate about political theology in the 1930s, but then clarifies that Metz "revived the term" and imbued it "with new meaning" (in reference to his 1968 essay discussed above).³⁷ Secondly, Metz, Moltmann, and Soelle all use "political theology" in a rather distinct sense from Schmitt. For these German theologians (and their English-speaking colleagues), political theology constituted a normative *theological* task or activity that sought to critically and constructively engage the secularization of Western society and the concomitant depoliticization of Christianity.

It is conceivable that our German theologians were *indirectly* influenced by Schmitt. It is possible that one or more of them were familiar with his *Political Theology*, or that they first came into

35. Kantorowicz, *King's Two Bodies*. Kantorowicz also used the term in a 1952 article called "Deus Per Naturam, Deus Per Gratiam: A Note on Mediaeval Political Theology." Oakley published an article in 1968 called "Jacobean Political Theology." He took the term from Kantorowicz and like him applied it to early modern political thought.

36. Both Obermann and Kantorowicz were educated in Germany. In regard to the latter, a number of scholars have perceived the direct influence of Schmitt. See Herrero, "On Political Theology," 1174–77. Though beyond the scope of the present work, one could productively make a distinction between the genealogy and usage of the concept "political theology" in continental European philosophical thought and North American theology, if not between political philosophy and theology more broadly.

37. Shelley's introduction to Soelle, *Political Theology*, xii.

contact with the term "political theology" by virtue of a German tradition indebted to Schmitt.[38] The fact remains, though, that Schmitt appears to have played no obviously meaningful role in the birth of political theology in the English-language context.[39] His *Political Theology*, after all, was not translated into English until 1985, well after Metz (with Moltmann) appears to have popularized the term amongst English-speaking theologians and imbued it with "new meaning."

In a final twist of irony, Schmitt actually revisited the issue of political theology precisely at the moment it was emerging as a phenomenon among German-speaking and English-speaking theologians. In 1970, he published his final book in German: *Politische Theologie II*. The irony is that it was not translated into English until 2008 and has all but been ignored by the field with which his name has become synonymous. Michael Hoelzl and Graham Ward assure us in their introduction to the English translation of *Political Theology* mark II that this one is "much more explicitly theological" than the first one, which they concede contained "a very limited amount of theology."[40] Montserrat Herrero notes that Schmitt understood "political theology as "a historical-juridical research field" rather than a theological or metaphysical one."[41]

The history of the term "political theology," in all its multifaceted glory, still awaits the historian's (now metaphorical) pen. While the origins of the term are indeed German, the German name most closely associated with the term, Carl Schmitt, appears to have played at best a marginal role in its emergence, at least as the art of political theology is conceived and practiced by professing Christians in the English-speaking world.

---

38. Schmitt's association with the Nazi Party provided ample motivation to avoid mentioning his name, even where a debt might have existed.

39. This does not mean to suggest that Schmitt is irrelevant to political theology today, nor unimportant. Indeed, if anything, interest in Schmitt's work in "political theology" has only grown in recent years, particularly in Europe.

40. Hoelzl and Ward's introduction to Schmitt, *Political Theology II*.

41. Herrero, "On Political Theology," 1177.

4

The Problematic Greek Roots of Contemporary Christian Political Theology[1]

CHRISTIAN POLITICAL THEOLOGY HAS a problem, which for the purposes of the present discussion I unimaginatively dub its "Greek problem." Michael Walzer identified the essence of this problem when he noted in his stimulating book *In God's Shadow* that "there is no political theory in the Bible," observing that "political theory is a Greek invention."[2] He added that the Bible does not appear to possess

> a clear conception of an autonomous or distinct political realm, nor of an activity called politics, nor of a status resembling Greek citizenship. And there is no systematic effort to think about this realm.[3]

Walzer, who is not a Christian theologian (political or otherwise), did not characterize this penetrating insight as a problem. He merely sought to make what he regarded as a factual observation.

1. Originally published as "The Problem with "Christian" Political Theology—It's Greek, Not Christian," *The New Polis*.
2. Walzer, *In God's Shadow*, xii.
3. Walzer, *In God's Shadow*, xii.

The Problematic Greek Roots of Christian Political Theology

I will endeavor to show that Walzer's observation represents a serious challenge for Christian political theology, of the type that takes seriously a Christian ontology and historical telos.[4] Furthermore, it is a problem that remains largely unacknowledged and unexamined by Christians.

The problem does not center on the fact that what many Christians hold to be either *the* source, or at the very least *a* source, of Christian political theology, namely the Bible, does *not* contain something that can be described unambiguously as an explicit, detailed, and comprehensive political theory. While it can be cogently argued that political theory is absent from the Bible, it cannot cogently be argued that politics per se is altogether absent (Walzer is well away of this). In fact, politics, or at least what we now designate under that conceptual category, is interwoven into the very narrative and text of Scripture, albeit not, as Walzer correctly points out, in a systematic and theoretically-minded manner. Take, for example, the political history of Israel that looms so large in the narrative of the Old Testament, or Paul's famous teaching about political authorities in the New Testament ("Let every person be subject to the governing authorities . . . " Rom 13:1), or again the political vocabulary repurposed for theological use in the New Testament, such as *ecclesia* (church) or *basileia* (kingdom).

The crux of the "Greek problem" is that the civilization that actually discovers and develops systematic political thought and which offers humanity its first detailed, sophisticated, and analytical descriptions of *actual* political regimes is pagan and Greek. That is to say that political thought originates with a people who had no knowledge of Yahweh, nor the texts that would subsequently come to shape Christian political theology. More to the point, pagan Greek political thought continues to exercise a profound and enduring influence over the way Christians and non-Christians alike conceive politics in the twenty-first century. The best evidence of this enduring influence, aside from the shape of Western liberal democratic institutions themselves, such as trial by a citizen jury,

---

4. See my definition of political theology in the introduction.

is the linguistic archeology of our political concepts. Hebrew has bequeathed English no political concept of any note, while Greek has given English some of its most fundamental political concepts and categories, including the very word "politics," and that which defines the type of polity in which this writer lives: democracy.

Christianity, in spite of the Bible's ostensible lack of interest in political theory, nevertheless developed its own civilization replete with its own political thought and political norms: Christendom and Byzantium. And herein lies the Greek problem: the distinctive Christian political idea that dominated both Christendom and Byzantium, notwithstanding their differences, was "divine kingship," with its corollaries "divine right to rule" and "Christian empire." And unlike democracy, to take but the most obvious example, "divine kingship" is a biblical idea. More specifically, it is an Israelite idea. Influential political theologian Oliver O'Donovan has argued that

> the hermeneutic principle that governs a Christian appeal to political categories within the Hebrew Scriptures is, simply, Israel itself . . . the governing principle is the kingly rule of God, expressed in Israel's corporate existence and brought to final effect in the life, death, and resurrection of Jesus.[5]

The political association in which God's kingly rule was understood by the Israelites to be active was not a liberal democracy. Rather, God's kingly rule manifested in what Norman Gottwald has described as a "tributary agrarian monarchy."[6]

To put the problem in its sharpest relief, then, the Western liberal political orders widely embraced and affirmed by what appears to be a majority of their Christian citizens today, both left and right, far more closely resemble what one finds in Aristotle's *The Athenian Constitution* than what one finds in 1 and 2 Kings, or indeed any other book of the Bible. Even more problematic is the fact that the Athenian and American Constitutions, which

5. O'Donovan, *Desire of the Nations*, 27.
6. Gottwald, *Politics of Ancient Israel*, 250.

effectively belong to the same species of polity, are not ostensibly compatible with either Christian monarchical empire or Israel's tributary agrarian monarchy, both of which belong to a different species of polity. Suffice to say, this very taxonomical distinction is also Greek.

For the sake of clarification, I make no claim that every aspect of Western liberal democracy is Greek, or concomitantly that none is Christian or biblical. Important elements of the former have been discarded or rejected for expressly Christian reasons, such as slavery, albeit in tragic fits and starts. Moreover, one can hardly discuss the genealogy of Western civilization with any pretense to seriousness in the absence of reference to the indelible influence of Rome. The fact of the matter is that one cannot draw a straight line from Athens to Washington, DC. There is a long Christian *interregnum* between Greek politics and contemporary American politics (or liberal democracy more broadly).

The nature and genealogy of contemporary Western liberal political order is admittedly more complex than I have allowed. Indeed, one could even treat contemporary Western liberal political order as the post-Christian outcrop of a Christianized Hellenic–Roman substratum.[7] Even so, the point still stands: we are much closer now to Greece than to Christendom, at least at the institutional level, and for most Christian citizens of Western polities this appears to be entirely unproblematic and unremarkable. To restate the problem with maxim clarity,

> Christians habitually embrace certain pagan Greek political concepts, principles, and norms, such as democracy, that are neither revealed in Christian Scripture nor emerge in Christendom or Byzantium, while at the same time rejecting (implicitly or explicitly) certain political ideas that are, namely, divine kingship and monarchical rule (in the Greek sense of the term).

---

7. Canning maintains that "the rich texture of political ideas in the Middle Ages was provided by the way in which the medieval versions of ultimately Greco-Roman and biblical concepts coexisted and interacted with purely medieval modes of thinking." Canning, *A History of Medieval Political Thought*, 1.

Christian Political Theology in an Age of Discontent

It is not my purpose to argue that the contemporary Christian embrace of democracy, constitutional rights, and citizen sovereignty is a mistake, or that these are not theologically defensible. My interest, rather, lies in the fact that the tension outlined directly above is not regarded as an *aporia* (in keeping with the Greek theme) by Christian political theologians, for I believe it has profound implications for the way Christians (ought to) think about the place of political institutions, norms, cultures, and histories in the divine economy. At a minimum, a Christian ought to be able to provide, or should at least attempt to provide, a coherent *theological* rationale for why Christians can and should embrace certain Greek pagan political principles while at the same time rejecting certain Judeo-Christian political principles.

Although the "Greek problem" has largely gone unremarked, I believe it plays a tacit role in the work of leading political theologians. Below I identify what I regard as three distinct strategies for resolving the "Greek problem" as I understand it. The aforementioned Oliver O'Donovan, who is English and Anglican, exemplifies one strategy, which attempts to ground Western liberal political order (or a version thereof) in Israel's and Christendom's political norms: "the unique covenant of Yhwh and Israel can be seen as a point of disclosure from which the nature of all political authority comes into view."[8] He argues that, "to display the liberal achievement correctly, we have to show it as the victory won by Christ over the nations' rulers."[9] He further avows that "the legal-constitutional conception is the essence of Christendom's legacy."[10] It is important to clarify that O'Donovan does not advocate an absolute return to either Israel's political norms or that of Christendom. Nor does he stand in opposition to democracy. Rather, he seeks to show that Western liberal political order is the direct product of Judeo-Christian political reflection and practice, with the Bible at its core. It is interesting to note, however, that there is no substantive discussion of Greek political theory and history

8. O'Donovan, *Desire of the Nations*, 45.
9. O'Donovan, *Desire of the Nations*, 229.
10. O'Donovan, *Desire of the Nations*, 240.

The Problematic Greek Roots of Christian Political Theology

or its enduring impact on Western liberal political order in any of O'Donovan's work in political theology. Moreover, he believes contemporary Western liberal political order is increasingly in danger of degeneracy precisely because it is moving further and further away from its Judeo-Christian foundations.

A second strategy is typified by Greek Orthodox thinker Christos Yannaras, who openly embraces aspects of Greek politics in the shape of a Helleno-Christian synthesis. Yannaras argues that the "struggle of the *polis* passed organically to the self-governing communities" in Byzantium and that the "ecclesia of the demos" found its metaphysical continuity in the "ecclesia of the believers."[11] Where O'Donovan sees contemporary Western liberal political norms at risk of degeneracy as a consequence of abandoning its biblio-Christendom roots, Yannaras sees it as long corrupted by its very *embrace* of Christendom and attendant *abandonment* of Greek political thought and praxis. He argues in his untranslated work *The Inhumanity of Rights* that the primacy of the individual in Western culture "does indeed represent progress in relation to the medieval West, but it is a tragic regression in comparison to the historical precedent of ancient Greek politics and a Helleno-Christian anthropology centered on personhood."[12] In contrast to O'Donovan, Yannaras all but ignores the political legacy of Israel and sees the seeds of the West's political salvation in a return to the Helleno-Christian political ideals put into effect in Athens and Constantinople.

For a third strategy, we turn to Stanley Hauerwas, who comes out of the Methodist tradition and (implicitly) resolves the "Greek problem" by repudiating the sanctity of Western liberal political order altogether along with its putative ancestry: Israel, Athens, Christendom, and Byzantium. Hauerwas instead calls for Christians to focus on being the church as a distinct political community and thus maintaining critical distance from secular politics: "I am not asking the church to withdraw, but rather to give up

11. Yannaras, "Συνεπάγεται αχρείωση ο αφελληνισμός" ["De-Hellenization Implies Degeneration"].

12. Yannaras, Ἡ ἀπανθρωπία τοῦ δικαιώματος [*The Inhumanity of Rights*], 47.

Christian Political Theology in an Age of Discontent

the presumptions of Constantinian power, particularly when those take the form of liberal universalism."[13] In *Resident Aliens* (with William Willimon), he writes:

> We believe both the conservative and liberal church, the so-called private and public church, are basically accommodationist (that is Constantinian) in their social ethic. Both assume wrongly that the American church's primary social task is to underwrite American democracy.[14]

As an aside, Hauerwas's critical ecclesial distance from the state arguably depends on the very thing it appears to reject: Western liberalism, including its Greek foundation, for it is probably only within the context of a liberal democracy that the church can safely maintain its independent and critical stance unhindered and unmolested.

The respective merits of these three strategies I leave open— they deserve more than the casual critique possible within the confines of this short discussion. Suffice to say, the positions here attributed to our respective cast are presented with much greater subtlety and sophistication than my schematic representations suggest. They do, however, serve to provide a proto-classification of strategies for resolving the "Greek problem": 1) Christian genealogy as an alternative to Greek genealogy (O'Donovan), Christian-Greek synthesis (Yannaras), and repudiation of both Greek and Christendom political thought and practice (Hauerwas). These distinct strategies for dealing with the West's Greek political legacy appear to indicate that the "Greek problem" represents an important demarcation within Christian political theology. Yet, none of the authors surveyed appears to recognize, or acknowledge, the existence of the "Greek problem" as I have characterized it.

It is difficult to explain the lack of *aporia* shown by today's Christian political theologians regarding the "Greek problem." But I wonder if it might have something to do with the narrow interests of theopolitical discourse, with its heavy emphasis on

---

13. Hauerwas, *After Christendom?*, 18.
14. Hauerwas and Willimon, *Resident Aliens*, 32.

The Problematic Greek Roots of Christian Political Theology

political commentary and activism, and its generally weak theoretical foundation, at least in comparison to related disciplines such as political science (certainly not without its own methodological and epistemological challenges).[15] In the current age, politics has become an all-consuming vortex of 24/7 media coverage saturated with an ever-multiplying cacophony of perspectives vomited or regurgitated into the public domain with the singular effect of eliciting instantaneous and unreflective reaction, opinion, and action in lieu of serious contemplation, argument, and dialogue. In that sense many Christians have perhaps simply fallen victim to the wider Western pathology of "politicizing ourselves to death."[16] Identifying and addressing political theology's central *aporias*, of which the "Greek problem" is but one, could serve to strengthen the theoretical foundations of political theology, on the one hand, and inoculate Christians from uncritically imbibing or following the cultural fashions and dogmas of their contingent political context and era, on the other.

---

15. This is a general criticism, not a specific criticism aimed at O'Donovan, Yannaras, or Hauerwas.

16. A play on the title of Neil Postman's masterful (and aptly titled for the present political moment) *Amusing Ourselves to Death: Public Discourse in the Age of Showbusiness*.

5

Christian Political Theology and Secular Political Philosophy

Conflict or Dialogue?[1]

WHAT IS THE DIFFERENCE between "political philosophy" and "political theology," aside from the name? In a straightforward sociological sense, the difference is that some scholars describe themselves, or are described by others, as "political philosophers," while others describe themselves, or are described by others, as "political theologians." Moreover, those so-described often find themselves institutionally separated—political philosophers in philosophy schools and political theologians in theology schools or seminaries. But if this is the only distinction, then it is a trivial one. Such differences do not, of themselves, resolve the question of whether political philosophy and political theology are substantively different endeavors or merely synonyms for the same endeavor. In this chapter, I examine whether there is a substantive difference by comparing and contrasting the work of political philosopher Joseph Raz and political theologian Oliver O'Donovan

1. Originally published as "Political Theology Must Be Engaged More Profoundly with Political Philosophy," *The Political Theology Network*.

on the topic of political authority. Both are regarded as leading thinkers on this topic in their respective fields.

Interestingly, O'Donovan and Raz's careers reflect the common functional separation of political philosophy and political theology in academia alluded to above. Raz was Professor of the Philosophy of Law at Oxford and Professor of Law at Columbia, while O'Donovan was Regius Professor of Moral and Pastoral theology at Oxford (substantially overlapping with Raz) and Professor of Christian Ethics and Practical Theology at the University of Edinburgh. I take Raz and O'Donovan to be characteristic of contemporary secular political philosophy and contemporary political theology, but not representative—both have their indigenous critics. My analysis is guided by three questions: 1) Are Raz and O'Donovan essentially talking about the same thing when they discuss "political authority"? 2) If they are, then what difference does the respective absence and presence of "theology" make to their accounts of political authority? 3) Does this distinction, to the extent that it exists, make dialogue between the two accounts feasible or infeasible?

It is difficult to provide succinct summaries of Raz's and O'Donovan's accounts of political authority without making a sacrificial offering on the altar of nuance. That said, brief expositions will suffice for the task at hand. To keep that task manageable, I will rely on Raz's essay "Authority and Justification" and O'Donovan's book *The Desire of the Nations*.

Raz proposes three theses which purport to explain how political authority is able to legitimately command obedience. These are named the "dependence thesis," the "preemptive thesis," and the "normal justification thesis." The "dependence thesis" argues that what *legitimate* political authority does in practice is rationally and objectively weigh up the "reasons which already independently apply to the subjects of the directives," and which "are relevant to their action in the circumstances covered by the directive."[2] In effect, a legitimate command is that which an individual would recognize as reasonable, appropriate, and legitimate independently

---

2. Raz, "Authority and Justification," 14.

of the person making the command. In other words, a command is legitimate to the extent that it is objectively and independently reasonable and justifiable, and not tied merely to the putative authority of the person or office issuing the command.

The "preemptive thesis" says that the dependent nature of *legitimate* political authority replaces the independent reasons upon which it is based.[3] That is to say that, where a directive is truly dependent in the sense described above, then the directive itself, rather than the dependent reasons upon which it is based, forms the grounds for compliance. The "normal justification thesis" explains how the "dependence" and "preemptive" theses can legitimize a particular political authority, such as a government. It maintains that an "alleged subject is likely better to comply with reasons that apply to him . . . if he accepts the directives of the alleged authority as authoritatively binding and tries to follow them."[4] Thus, where the "subject" is more likely to do the right thing by following a political authority that he or she has grounds to believe will consistently issue directives based on objective reasons that apply to the subject independently of that authority's directive, the subject can morally obey that political authority.

Although O'Donovan's account of political authority does not neatly divide into an explicit threefold schema per Raz, it does nevertheless depend on three identifiable theses which I name for the purposes of comparative analysis as follows: the "normative political authority thesis," the "providence thesis," and the "re-authorization thesis." O'Donovan contends that political authority can only be understood within the context of an "account of the reign of God."[5] He maintains that "the unique covenant of Yhwh and Israel can be seen as a point of disclosure from which the nature of all political authority comes into view."[6] The essence of political authority is revealed in the way that Israel mediated God's kingship, most particularly during the Davidic monarchy.

---

3. Raz, "Authority and Justification," 10.
4. Raz, "Authority and Justification," 19.
5. O'Donovan, *Desire of the Nations*, 19.
6. O'Donovan, *Desire of the Nations*, 45.

Christian Political Theology and Secular Political Philosophy

The essence of political authority consists of the conjunction of power, the execution of right, and the perpetuation of tradition in one coordinated agency.[7] The purpose of this conjunction, and hence of political authority, is the enactment of justice.

The "providence thesis" says that the fact that any regime can come to hold and continue to hold political authority (as defined above) is "a work of divine providence in history, not a mere accomplishment of the human task of political service."[8] Finally, the "re-authorization thesis" argues that the exaltation of Christ and the emergence of the church presage a re-authorization of political authority such that in the post-Easter phase of salvation-history judgment, and judgment alone, forms the sole legitimate function of political authority.[9] Judgment denotes "an act of moral discrimination that pronounces upon a preceding act or existing state of affairs to establish a new public context.'"[10] O'Donovan claims to find support for the "re-authorization thesis" in Rom 13:1-7.

That Raz and O'Donovan provide two very different accounts of political authority hardly needs emphasizing. But given diversity of opinion is *de rigueur* in both political philosophy and political theology, the mere fact that their accounts differ does not settle the question of whether those accounts necessarily belong to two different discourses. The first thing to note is that it is quite clear that Raz and O'Donovan are broadly addressing the same phenomenon: political authority. They may define this central concept differently, but there is clearly a degree of conceptual convergence. Both make it clear that political authority relates to the activity of governments, for instance. Furthermore, Raz's "directives" and O'Donovan's "judgments" appear to be cognate given they both describe activities performed by governments that purport to command obedience. However, while there are grounds to think that both analyze the same phenomenon, O'Donovan's account contains *theological* concepts that are completely absent from Raz's

7. O'Donovan, *Desire of the Nations*, 46.
8. O'Donovan, *Desire of the Nations*, 46.
9. O'Donovan, *Desire of the Nations*, 151.
10. O'Donovan, *Ways of Judgment*, 7.

account. O'Donovan's account of political authority includes, and is dependent on, concepts such as God's divine kingship, Israel's covenant with God, providence, and Christ's exaltation. Raz's account, by way of contrast, neither mentions God nor any thing that could be described as a theological concept. Nor is there any reference to Scripture or Israel in his account (Raz, interestingly enough, is Israeli). In fact, Raz's account of political authority does not even presuppose the existence of a God, Christian or otherwise. His is an entirely naturalistic account of political authority. The absence of theological conceptuality found in Raz is characteristic of much contemporary political philosophy.

It is possible to infer one of two things from the absence of theological concepts in Raz's account of political authority: either such concepts are regarded as untrue and therefore irrelevant to the phenomenon of political authority, or they are regarded as true, or possibly true, but not necessary to explain the phenomenon of political authority. This inference suggests the existence of a substantive difference between political philosophy and political theology: the theological conceptuality that is characteristic of political theology is alien to the conceptuality of political philosophy, even though they share a common political vocabulary and ostensibly investigate common social phenomena. But there is an even more substantive difference, which can be profitably dubbed "epistemic methodology."

One of the interesting contrasts between Raz and O'Donovan is that Raz finds the existence of political authority, i.e., the ontology of political authority, entirely unproblematic. Political authority simply exists, like any other social phenomenon, and the only thing begging explanation is how it works and what its normative function is. Raz's methodology could thus be described as empirical-rational. He applies rational analysis to what can be observed in relation to the phenomenon conventionally denoted by usage of the English term authority. He takes an axiomatic view of the ability of human reason to reliably describe and explain the phenomenon of political authority. O'Donovan, on the other hand, believes that the existence of political authority is problematic and

Christian Political Theology and Secular Political Philosophy

begs explanation. In fact, he believes it is unintelligible without reference to God, and that this, moreover, is a weakness of modern secular contractarian theories of political authority. While he too employs empirical observation and rational analysis, he additionally relies on theological concepts, revealed historical texts (Scripture), and the notion of salvation-history to help identify and explain both the essence and normative function of political authority.

This difference in epistemic methodology is significant as it gives political philosophy and political theology a different framework for judging the validity of political theories. This might help explain why the two fields appear to have organically developed into largely separate discourses. But does this necessarily preclude dialogue? The fact that political philosophy and political theology ostensibly investigate the same phenomena creates a prima facie basis for dialogue. Moreover, the different epistemic methodologies with the different, albeit to some extent overlapping, conceptualities they generate do not necessarily undermine that basis. Political philosophers, after all, entertain a wide variety of theoretical and methodological approaches. Influential philosophical anarchist Robert Wolff argues *pace* Raz that the anarchist "will never view the commands of the state as *legitimate*, as having binding moral force."[11] But this contrary view has not stopped political philosophers from taking Wolff seriously and engaging his arguments. It is important to note, however, that Wolff reaches his anarchist conclusions through the same epistemic methodology as Raz. His account of political authority is naturalistic and empirical-rational, and like Raz he ignores theological concepts.

The question, then, is this: can political philosophers take seriously the arguments advanced by political theologians in relation to phenomena investigated by both parties in spite of political theologians using an epistemic methodology and theological concepts that the political philosopher might not regard as credible or even relevant? This really boils down to attitude. There is nothing

---

11. Wolff, "Conflict between Authority and Autonomy," 29. Emphasis original.

in principle to stop an atheist or agnostic political philosopher critically engaging the work of a political theologian except prejudice. If current trends in the attitudes of the Western intelligentsia towards Christian belief are anything to go by, then prejudice may indeed be an obstacle. Atheist scholars of the Richard Dawkins variety simply do not believe an intelligent human being can hold Christian beliefs, in which case there is no point reading, let alone taking seriously, anything purporting to be theological scholarship. One does sadly encounter a mirror prejudice among some Christians: the atheist couldn't possibly say anything illuminating for theology.

But not all atheist and agnostic political philosophers share Dawkins's polemical attitude towards theology. It is possible, therefore, that the absence of any reference to, or engagement with, political theology on the part of many contemporary political philosophers may simply be the product of perceptions about relevance rather than prejudice. Whatever its reason, this silence indicates that it may fall to political theologians to initiate dialogue by demonstrating that their work is both credible and relevant to the work of political philosophers. Political theologians must provide genuine insights into political reality if they expect political philosophers to take their work seriously.

Political theology is arguably more open to political philosophy than vice versa. It is not uncommon to find references to the work of contemporary political philosophers in political theology. And there are, of course, *Christian* philosophers of prominence within academia—Alvin Plantinga, Nicholas Wolterstorff, Charles Taylor, and Alasdair MacIntyre immediately come to mind in the English-speaking context. One can even find atheists (at least in the continental tradition) who show some interest in political theology, e.g., Slavoj Žižek and Giorgio Agamben. But it is difficult to think of contemporary political theologians, at least those who describe themselves as such, who have come to the attention of non-Christian political philosophers, let alone left their mark in the field of political philosophy. Again, to some extent this might be the product of prejudice. But as long as engagement of secular political philosophy on the part of political theologians amounts to little more than the occasional citation of a political philosopher, we should hold out no great ambition for meaningful critical dialogue. What is required is deep and sustained engagement.

The reality is that scholars of any stripe are far more likely to take note of work that substantively engages their own work, or that intersects with its interests and arguments. If prejudice is an obstacle, then the way to remove it is for political theologians to show that they can critically and insightfully engage the best work political philosophy has to offer without parking their theological commitments at the door. This is not to suggest that political theology must conform to the interests, questions, and predilections of contemporary political philosophy. It is simply a clarion call for political theologians to engage contemporary political philosophy more deeply and more often than is currently the case. Such an engagement would give political theologians the opportunity to demonstrate to non-Christian political philosophers that political theology can credibly challenge, illuminate, and constructively contribute to political philosophy, even if the epistemic methodology of the former ultimately fails to find favor with the latter.

6

Reason and Nature

The Political Theology of Thomas Hobbes[1]

IN THIS CHAPTER I explore the political theology of Thomas Hobbes in his iconic book *Leviathan*. This is a self-conscious exercise in anachronism. Suffice to say, Hobbes was not aware that he had something called a "political theology" or that in writing *Leviathan* he expounded such a thing. But Hobbes wrote at a time when political philosophy proceeded from explicit theological commitments—and took for granted the relevance of Christian Scripture—to political theory. In short, it was an age which had no need for a discrete activity called political theology. What's more, any contemporary definition of political theology brings *Leviathan* comfortably within its scope.

Hobbes is probably best known for his famous, and famously pessimistic, anthropology, which posited that the natural "condition of Man ... is a condition of Warre of every one against every one."[2] The remedy he proposed to the pre-political insecurity of humankind has grown ever more controversial with the passage

---

1. Originally published as "Delegated Divine Rule"—On Hobbes and the Origins of Political Theology, *The Political Theology Network*.
2. Hobbes, *Leviathan*, I.14.

Reason and Nature

of time, for within the context of modern political categories it sits rather awkwardly and embarrassingly in the orbit of authoritarianism. *Leviathan* was "occasioned by the disorders of the present time," which is to say the English civil war of 1642–1651, and Hobbes's anthropology must be read against this backdrop.[3] He saw getting humans "out from that miserable condition of Warre" as the end of politics. That end required a "common power" that could keep them "in awe, and tye them by feare of punishment to the performance of their Covenants."[4] Hobbes baptized this common power the "sovereign," which in modern parlance we might prefer to call the "government."

The essence of Hobbes's theory of government lay in the notion that men

> conferre all their power and strength upon one Man, or upon one Assembly of men, that may reduce all their Wills, by plurality of voices, unto one Will: which is as much as to say, to appoint one man, or Assembly of men, to beare their Person; and every one to owne, and acknowledge himselfe to be Author of whatsoever he that so beareth their Person, shall Act, or cause to be Acted . . . and therein to submit their Wills, every one to his Will, and their Judgments, to his Judgment.[5]

Hobbes described a "Multitude so united in one Person" as "that great LEVIATHAN," bequeathing political thought one of its most memorable and enduring metaphors. This leviathan acted as "that *Mortall God*, to which wee owe under the *Immortall God*, our peace and defence."[6]

The most controversial aspect of Hobbes's account of government was the idea that nothing this mortal God "can doe to a Subject, on what pretence soever, can properly be called Injustice, or Injury; because every Subject is Author of every act the Soveraign

---

3. Hobbes, *Leviathan*, 728.
4. Hobbes, *Leviathan*, II.17.
5. Hobbes, *Leviathan*, II.17.
6. Hobbes, *Leviathan*, II.17.

doth."⁷ The moral justification for vesting such unbridled power in one man or assembly of men, aside from the liberation of man from his natural state of war, rests on the notion of "covenant," an idea which Hobbes took from the Abrahamic covenant of the Old Testament. Hobbes believed that men voluntarily enter into mutual covenant, implying therefore that people have in some sense consented to the type of sovereign power for which he advocated.

Hobbes made a distinction between his "discourse" on a commonwealth and his "discourse" on a Christian commonwealth (treated separately in different parts of the book). The methodology he adopted in the case of the former was to "derive . . . the Rights of Soveraigne Power, and the duty of Subjects hitherto, from the Principles of Nature onely . . . that is to say, from the nature of Men, known to us by Experience."⁸ In the case of the latter, "there dependeth much upon Supernaturall Revelations of the Will of God."⁹ In reality both discourses involve wide-ranging discussion of God, Scripture, and Christian doctrine. This is because Hobbes takes God to be the author of the natural laws from which he develops his principles of sovereign power in the first place. God's sovereign power and rule are manifest in and realized through the natural laws that Hobbes says govern the political order. By natural laws Hobbes really means moral laws. God's sovereignty is therefore a foundational idea in Hobbes's political thought. The all-powerful sovereign who can do no wrong to his subjects is still subject to God's own sovereign power. He thus exercises a delegated power as God's "lieutenant" and is "bound thereby to observe the laws of Nature."¹⁰ Indeed, one of the primary tasks of the sovereign, according to Hobbes, is to impel men to live in accordance with the laws of nature.

The fundamental theopolitical principle at work in *Leviathan*, then, is that of "delegated divine rule."¹¹ In theory, God rules

7. Hobbes, *Leviathan*, II.21.
8. Hobbes, *Leviathan*, III.32.
9. Hobbes, *Leviathan*, III.32.
10. Hobbes, *Leviathan*, II.21.
11. My term, not Hobbes's.

the world through reason and the laws of nature. In practice, God rules through mortal human gods whose power is constrained only by their duty to rule according to the "dictates" of reason. The senses, experience, and reason, Hobbes argued, are "the talents which . . . [God] . . . hath put into our hands" to be "employed in the purchase of Justice, Peace, and, true Religion."[12] Politics is therefore principally a rational endeavor, where reason performs the function of discerning the laws of nature. We might venture heuristically to characterize Hobbes's theopolitical method as "naturalistic rationalism."

Hobbes made a distinction between natural laws, which were eternal, and positive laws (also civil laws), which were made by the will of the sovereign. Positive laws could also be divine and revealed.[13] But in reality, divine positive laws were simply those deemed compatible with reason and natural law by the sovereign, thus making the sovereign the sole arbiter of divine law in practice. Hobbes conceded that there were "many things in Gods Word above Reason; that is to say, which cannot by naturall reason be either demonstrated, or confuted."[14] However, he maintained that any ostensible clash between reason and revelation was merely indicative of either "unskilfull Interpretation, or erroneous Ratiocination."[15] In other words, where there was a conflict between reason and revelation, one should err on the side of reason.

The primacy of reason over revelation can be seen in the criterion Hobbes laid out for determining the validity of divine law: "in all things not contrary to the Morall Law, (that is to say, to the Law of Nature,) all Subjects are bound to obey that for divine Law, which is declared to be so, by the Lawes of the Commonwealth."[16] Thus the divine law revealed in Scripture had to justify its compatibility with reason and natural law before it could be said to command obedience, and then only on the authority of the sover-

12. Hobbes, *Leviathan*, III.32.
13. Hobbes, *Leviathan*, II.26
14. Hobbes, *Leviathan*, III.32.
15. Hobbes, *Leviathan*, III.32.
16. Hobbes, *Leviathan*, II.26.

eign. It is important to note that Hobbes (a member of the Church of England) identified the sovereign with the church, because the latter "consisteth in Christian men, united in one Christian Soveraign."[17]

The priority of reason in Hobbes's political vision is particularly evident in the way he deals with the kingdom of God, one of the great preoccupations of *Leviathan*. The kingdom of God represents one of the book's more difficult ideas to decipher. It assumes different senses that are not always clearly or coherently related. Notwithstanding this complexity, one constant shines forth: the kingdom of God is "literal," i.e., it only ever refers in Scripture to a tangible, earthly kingdom. In the first instance, the kingdom of God represents God's rule over the natural world, captured in Hobbes's pregnant phrase: "the naturall Kingdome of God": "Naturall, wherein he governeth as many of Mankind as acknowledge his Providence, by the naturall Dictates of Right Reason."[18] Hobbes even regarded obedience to God's natural laws as "the greatest worship of all."[19] He also understood the kingdom of God to relate to Israel, the beginning of which he quixotically dates to the Mosaic period and ends paradoxically with the rise of the monarchy inaugurated by the usurper Saul. But Hobbes then extends the notion of the kingdom of God so that it becomes identifiable with the civil commonwealth, which is to say that the kingdom of God is actually the Hobbesian leviathan:

> It is therefore manifest enough . . . that by the *Kingdome of God*, is properly meant a Common-wealth, instituted (by the consent of those which were to be subject thereto) for their Civill Government, and the regulating of their behavior.[20]

Hobbes even construes "salvation" as the establishment and maintenance of a civil commonwealth: "to be saved, is to be secured,

---

17. Hobbes, *Leviathan*, III.33.
18. Hobbes, *Leviathan*, II.31.
19. Hobbes, *Leviathan*, II.31.
20. Hobbes, *Leviathan*, III.35.

either respectively, against special Evills, or absolutely against all Evill."[21] And given "kingdom" represents "an estate ordained by men for their perpetuall security against enemies, and want . . . it seemeth that this Salvation should be on Earth."[22]

The advent of Christ, for Hobbes, renewed the Abrahamic covenant breached by the rise of the Israelite monarchy, thus restoring the kingdom of God in the form of the Christian commonwealth. In the future, Christ will return to inaugurate and rule the "kingdom of Christ" which will assume the form of a real, tangible civil kingdom on earth (Hobbes understood heavenly reward and the punishment of hell as referring to experiences here on earth).

The more one reflects on the theopolitical logic of *Leviathan* the more one gains the impression that Hobbes's intent was not to expound a theologically-warranted polity so much as to relegate the role of theology to the very margins of politics. For Hobbes completely subordinates revelation to the God of reason. The kingdom of God is subordinated to the civil commonwealth. Divine law is subordinated to the civil legislative authority of the sovereign. Moreover, salvation is reduced to the peace and security wrought by a mortal god in the person of the sovereign. It is not vested in the risen Son of the immortal God in accordance with orthodox Christian belief.

Political context is destiny in the case of political theory, and it is not difficult to infer a motive for Hobbes's subjugation of revelation and theology to a Christian civil government. The royalist Hobbes was writing during England's abortive Christian Republic (the Commonwealth of England), whose regicidal Lord Protector claimed to to be acting on direct divine inspiration.[23] Hobbes thought men like Cromwell "pretended for their disobedience to their Sovereign, a new Covenant, made, not with men, but with God."[24]

---

21. Hobbes, *Leviathan*, III.38.

22. Hobbes, *Leviathan*, III.38.

23. Worden observes that "the nearest thing to a clear division between the two sides [in the civil war] is a religious one." Worden, *English Civil Wars*, ch. 2.

24. Hobbes, *Leviathan*, II.18.

Given Hobbes is indisputably regarded as a giant in the pantheon of Western political thought, *and* on any definition his magnum opus qualifies as a work in political theology, why has he largely been ignored by contemporary political theologians? Several possibilities suggest themselves. One possibility is that Hobbes's political vision of subjects surrendering their will to a mighty sovereign power is so out of step with today's democratic ideals that *Leviathan* is not deemed a credible or fruitful "conversation partner" for contemporary political theologians. Another possibility is that the unorthodoxy of much of Hobbes's theology and biblical exegesis makes the political arguments derived thereof suspect for political theologians trying to marry orthodox Christian theological doctrine to political reality. Interestingly, Hobbes was conscious that some of his views were discordant with the theological orthodoxy of his own day, admitting, for instance, that his "doctrine" of the kingdom of God would "appear to most men a novelty."[25] A final possibility is that the secular appropriation of Hobbes has been so complete that many theologians are simply unaware that one of the Western tradition's most seminal political thinkers wrestled with the intersection between revelation, natural law, divine sovereignty, and political authority.

To explore this final possibility further, I embark on a brief discussion of two contrasting perspectives on Hobbes's legacy to political theology offered by Oliver O'Donovan and Mark Lilla. In *The Desire of the Nations*, O'Donovan recounts his "excitement" at discovering in *Leviathan* "a Great Tradition of political theology, almost unknown to today's theologians."[26] He thought "Hobbes the theologian" could do with a "rehabilitation." But he also acknowledged that Hobbes marked "the point at which the Tradition . . . abdicated, leaving the characteristic problems of modern political theory in its wake," by which O'Donovan meant the point at which political philosophy and theology were rent asunder.[27] Lilla, by way of contrast, writing in *The Stillborn God*, thinks

---

25. Hobbes, *Leviathan*, III.38.
26. O'Donovan, *Desire of the Nations*, xi.
27. O'Donovan, *Desire of the Nations*, xi.

Leviathan "contains the most devastating attack on Christian political theology ever undertaken."[28] He credits Hobbes with charting a course towards Western society's escape from the nefarious embrace of political theology, an embrace which he thinks has perverted human politics since time immemorial.

Is Hobbes, then, the final great political theologian of the Christian tradition or its executioner? The truth is probably to be found in the Aristotelian virtue of a mean between two extremes. By construing politics as a matter of will, constrained only by the law of nature as discerned by reason, Hobbes undoubtedly laid the foundations for a purely secular account of political order and government (secular in the modern sense of non-sacred). For once alternative non-divine explanations for the existence of man, reason, and nature became available, political thinkers quickly grasped that there was no longer even a need to cling to the transitional view of what Lilla aptly called *deus absconditus*.[29] But this speaks to the long-term impact of *Leviathan*, not to the mind of Hobbes. Lilla writes as though Hobbes intended to consciously destroy political theology altogether, as if he only engaged Scripture and theological doctrine as a cunning sop to the superstitious society around him, motivated solely by the desire to make his radically secular political vision more palatable. However, there is every indication that Hobbes's idiosyncratic theology and hermeneutic emerged from a genuinely-held Christian faith. When he referred to God as "creator," he does not appear to have done so metaphorically, nor when he spoke of Jesus' future reign on Earth. While I believe Hobbes did seek to minimize the political influence of Scripture, theology, and the divines of his day, his motive appears to have been to banish what he regarded as theological superstition from the field of politics, not erase the Christian God from the scene altogether. It is also far from clear that Hobbes would greet the death of political theology with the same alacrity as Lilla clearly does.

28. Lilla, *Stillborn God*, 75.
29. Lilla, *Stillborn God*, 26.

In the case of O'Donovan, I think he has probably underestimated the extent to which Hobbes sought to subjugate theology to politics. In *The Desire of the Nations*, O'Donovan argues that God exercises his kingly rule providentially through the judgments made by secular governments in the light of Christ's triumph over the nations. *Leviathan*, I think, inverts this order. Hobbes essentially argues for the triumph of the nation—the civil commonwealth—over Christ. *Leviathan* assures us that Christ will come again one day to rule. In the meantime, the task of politics falls to humans and is a matter of freedom, will, and reason, albeit united in one Christian body under the sovereign. In any event, O'Donovan and Lilla agree that Hobbes constitutes a pivotal figure in the history of political theology, and I find myself in agreement. Irrespective of where one stands with regard to Hobbes's legacy, *Leviathan* deserves to be treated as a serious work in political theology.

7

"Thank You Lord Jesus for President Trump"
The Apostolic Political Theology of American Evangelicalism[1]

THE DISCOMBOBULATING ARRIVAL OF Trumpism has consigned many a conventional political wisdom to the wastelands of the now discredited art of political prognostication. The Trump presidency, along with its cousin Brexit, has left political analysis in a state of flummox. Commentators, pundits, and soothsayers across the ever-expanding political spectrum vie in what feels like a vain effort to make sense of the beguiling currents of change evidently afflicting Western civilization. All and sundry agree that seismic political change is afoot. Few, if any, however, have been able to cogently point to its root causes, let alone its obscure destination.

The conventional wisdoms of Christian political theology are no less affected by this unnamed contemporary political revolution than those of their estranged secular counterparts. The fact, for example, that a majority of evangelical voters cast their ballot for the supposedly unelectable Trump, and that those voters have

[1]. Originally published as ""Thank You Lord Jesus for President Trump"—Apostolic Theology and the Evangelical Vote," *The Political Theology Network*.

doggedly stuck by him through thick and thin, asks searching questions of the political theologian (including the evangelical political theologian). Among them is "what theopolitical rationale is at work in the evangelical embrace of the Trump presidency?" In an attempt to begin to answer this question, I examine in this chapter the theopolitical assumptions that appear to underpin an iconic image from 2015, that of a woman holding aloft a sign at a Trump campaign rally with the slogan: "Thank You, Lord Jesus, For President Trump."[2]

It would be unduly facile to suggest that a single slogan could encapsulate the sentiment of the millions of Christian voters who helped see Trump to victory, and I suffer from no such delusion. However, I believe that the implicit political theology underpinning that simple slogan illuminates something important about contemporary American evangelical political theology. At first glance, the slogan will no doubt strike Christian members of that increasing magnet of opprobrium "the elite" as hopelessly naïve and simplistic, although there is admittedly a limit to the erudition one can reasonably display in the constrained format of a slogan. The image unsurprisingly met with disdain on that contemporary vehicle of scorn otherwise known as "social media."[3]

Still, there are interesting theopolitical assumptions that can be inferred from the notion that Jesus might have ordained, or perhaps facilitated, the Trump presidency.[4] For the purposes of the present discussion I term this underlying assumption: "apostolic political theology." Here I mean "apostolic" in the Greek sense

---

2. The photo, which went viral at the time (not just because of the sign), was taken by Mark Wallheiser at a campaign rally in Mobile, Alabama, on August 21, 2015. Cillizza, "Let's Break Down This Amazing Donald Trump Picture."

3. Online responses described the photo as "creepy," "hilarious," and "terrifying," Abramovitch, "Donald Trump Viral Baby Photo."

4. Indeed, such a view has been expressed explicitly by some Christians (including evangelicals). A movie called *The Trump Prophecy*, which claims that Trump's election "was an act of God, who chose [Trump] . . . to restore America's moral values," screened in 2018 (Sherwood, "The Chosen One?"). Franklin Graham has indicated that he believes God put Trump in office for a "purpose." *USA Today*, "Billy Graham's Son."

of *apostolos*, i.e., someone sent for a specific purpose or mission. An "apostolic political theology" rests on the notion that God, or in this case Jesus, sends or raises up specific political leaders at specific times and in specific places for specific purposes. While I make no suggestion that "apostolic political theology" is representative of all evangelical political theology in America, it does strike this external observer of the drama of American politics as characteristically American.

"Apostolic political theology" has a plausible theological basis. The New Testament teaches that political authority comes from God. The most famous such passage is found in Paul's letter to the church at Rome, in which he suggests that "those authorities that exist have been instituted by God" (13:1). In John's Gospel, Jesus tells Pilate: "You would have no power over me unless it had been given you from above" (19:11). The Old Testament presents us with instances of specific rulers being used to perform God's purposes, including enemies of God's people. In 1 Kgs 11:14, for instance, we find the following passage: "Then the Lord raised up an adversary against Solomon, Hadad the Edomite." Prov 8:15 says: "By me kings reign, and rulers decree what is just." Setting aside the question of Trump for the moment, the notion that God might raise up a specific ruler clearly has some biblical basis, and would not be a foreign notion to Christians in bygone eras. Indeed, the notion that all rulers receive their office from God has been a dominant paradigm throughout Christian history, even if it is a source of contention today.

Returning to the sign, however, it is worth noting that it did not say, per Proverbs: "Thank You, Lord Jesus, For Raising Up Just Rulers." Moreover, it appeared during the primaries. It thus seems to claim much more than the generic notion that "all authority comes from God." Implicit in the slogan is the idea that it is possible for the Christian to discern God's anointment of a particular *candidate* for political office in the context of democratic elections. Calvin believed all magistrates, including the tyrant, owed their office to God, and that all rulers should be obeyed provided they did not command anything against God.⁵ But Calvin did not have to contend with what I will call the "discernment problem." The "discernment problem" is this: on what basis can the Christian *reasonably* and *reliably* discern that candidate *x* is God's anointed candidate in a democratic election? In Calvin's day, of course, most people were not given the opportunity to choose their magistrates. Implicit in the idea that God anoints a specific candidate in a democratic election is the notion that other candidates are not duly anointed, thus making elections a contest between God's candidate and those who presumably would seek to thwart, wittingly or unwittingly, God's purposes. As an aside, it is worth noting that applying Calvin's view of politics to contemporary America would also appear to require the evangelical to wave a sign saying: "Thank You, Lord Jesus, For the Eight Years of the Obama Presidency." All magistrates are appointed by God, after all. Even a liberal (progressive) tyrant, to extend Calvin's logic, "possess[es] the sacred majesty with which [God] has invested legitimate authority" and is "raised up by him to punish the iniquity of the people."⁶

The central problem for an "apostolic political theology" of the sort implicit in the aforementioned slogan is the intractable difficulty of identifying an *objective* theological basis for making the discernment that Trump was God's chosen candidate in the 2016 presidential election. To state the obvious, the Bible is silent about the United States of America, presidential elections, and Donald Trump. This is not to say that Trump might not be God's anointed leader of America. It is to point to the fact that it is exceedingly difficult to see how anyone could know this short of a personal encounter with a burning bush. Nor is it to suggest that there do not exist reasons that could allow a Christian to vote for Trump in good conscience. It is to suggest that it is difficult to identify an objective *theological* basis upon which a voter might conclude that Trump is anointed by Jesus.

Polling suggests that the issue of abortion was determinative of much evangelical support for Trump, particularly in the context

5. Calvin, "On Civil Government," 4.20.32. See chapter 8 for a closer look at the Calvinist roots of contemporary evangelical political theology in America.
6. Calvin, "On Civil Government," 4.20.25.

of a vacancy in the Supreme Court going into the election. But does a candidate's position on abortion really bridge the "discernment problem"? If we accept that a candidate's stance on abortion, or any other single issue for that matter, is a sound Christian criterion upon which to make a faithful voting decision, does it necessarily follow that Trump is God's man? He was not the only Republican nominee with a pro-life stance. In fact, his stance on the issue had been less consistent and less strident than some of his rivals in the Republican primaries (although it must be conceded that it was much stronger than any likely Democratic opponent in the election). Moreover, any number of Republican primary contenders was bound to appoint a judicial conservative to the Supreme Court. In any case, the very idea that God's approval or anointment of a candidate in a democratic election could be determined by that candidate's campaign rhetoric on just one solitary issue of importance strains credulity.

In reality, all voting decisions are unavoidably subjective given there is no guarantee how a candidate will act in office once elected, especially when voters must come to a decision amidst the relentless assault of alternatively beatifying and demonizing rhetoric from candidates, opponents, and acolytes on either side of an electoral race. So there is reason to be skeptical that a criterion could be identified and objectively applied capable of satisfactorily resolving the "discernment problem."

To be clear, the problem is not that voting involves subjective judgment. That is unavoidable. The issue is whether the intrinsic subjectivity involved in making electoral judgments constitutes a suitable foundation for making categorical claims regarding the divine anointment of one particular candidate. Political history is littered with the corpses of false prophets and failed political messiahs. The hope German Christians earnestly invested in Adolf Hitler in the 1930s looks tragically absurd with the benefit of hindsight. But in truth, no one can be entirely sure what they are purchasing in the supermarket of politics. Germans genuinely yearned for a savior at the time Hitler rose to power and he promised to make Germany great again. Contrary to the protestations of partisan political animals, no US president (or political leader of any nation for that matter) is ever unambiguously good or bad, a simple success or failure. They are inevitably a frustrating mix of the two, with some enjoying a greater measure of success and others failure.[7] The office is occupied by mere mortals, not gods, or even demigods.[8]

It is one thing, then, to believe that God is the Lord of history and that he has a greater or lesser providential role in politics. One may even humbly engage in speculation about the hand of God *post eventum*. But given the inscrutable nature of political futures from the human vantage point, it is another thing entirely to presume to be able to discern God's purpose right down to identifying his anointed candidate in a particular presidential race. That is prophecy, not political analysis.

Whatever conclusion one draws regarding the "discernment problem" and the particular discernment made by many Christian voters in relation to Donald Trump, there is a deeper question about the roots of America's apparent "apostolic political theology." It appears to stem from the ideal cherished by many Christians that America is itself an apostolic nation, anointed to perform a special divine mission in global history. If America is, as Puritan settler John Winthrop famously preached, "a city upon a hill,"[9] then the search for a presidential apostle is not only plausible, but perhaps necessary, particularly at a time when the Republic appears to many of its Bible-reading citizens to have abandoned its manifest destiny.

---

7. Barth made a similar point in relation to states, observing (in the wake of World War II) that they are "always a curious mixture" of both good and bad. Barth, "Christian Community and the Civil Community," 164.

8. See chapter 12 for my discussion of the natural constraints on human political capacity.

9. Winthrop, "A Model of Christian Charity."

8

The Calvinist Roots of Evangelical Support for President Trump[1]

AN ENDURING FASCINATION IN the age of Trump has been the apparently unflappable pillar of evangelical support that helped put him in office. For well-documented reasons it hardly bears repeating that Trump is a rather unlikely evangelical hero. The prevailing narrative attributes the impetus behind this support to concerns over Supreme Court nominations and the protection of religious freedoms. But these two signal issues of themselves do not explain the theopolitical logic operative in Trump's steadfast evangelical support.

For the purposes of probing the *possible* theopolitical logic that has facilitated evangelical support for Trump, beyond the epiphenomena of the Supreme Court and religious freedom, I propose to examine Calvin's political theology on the hypothesis that it will prove illuminating. This exercise does not pretend to divine what Calvin himself might have thought about the Trump presidency. What follows is my own analysis and application of Calvin's theopolitical vision to circumstances unknown to Calvin. The ambition is no greater than suggesting a lens through which a

1. Originally published as "A Calvinist Take on Why Evangelicals Support Donald Trump," *The Political Theology Network*.

possible theopolitical logic might be discerned in evangelical support for Trump.

Suffice to say, not all evangelicals support Trump and some erstwhile supporters have long recanted. It also goes without saying that not all evangelicals are Calvinists. Moreover, I make no presumption that those Trump-supporting evangelicals who *are* deeply influenced by Calvin's theology arrived at that support after scrutinizing Calvin's political theology in book IV, chapter 20 of the *Institutes*—"On Civil Government," the text examined below. Calvin, however, is an important and revered figure for many evangelicals, in which case it seems reasonable to posit that his political thought might have shaped to some extent contemporary American evangelical political theology. Finally, what follows is an exercise in applied historical political theology with no greater ambition than elucidation. To this end I approach both Calvin and evangelical support for Trump from a neutral perspective, to the extent to which a neutral perspective on any topic is humanly possible.

Calvin believed that humans are subject to two kinds of government: "the kingdom of Christ," which "is situated in the soul, or the inner man, and relates to eternal life," and the "civil government," which "relates to civil justice and the regulation of the external conduct."[2] Although these two governments are not at "variance" with one another, Calvin nevertheless understood them to be "things very different and remote from each other."[3] He went so far as to describe it as a "Jewish folly . . . to seek and include the kingdom of Christ under the elements of this world" (advice unheeded by Hobbes, as we saw in chapter 6).[4]

---

2. Calvin, "On Civil Government," 4.20.1.

3. Calvin, "On Civil Government," 4.20.1. This idea is also found in Luther: "Therefore care must be taken to keep these two governments distinct, and both must be allowed to continue [their work], the one to make [people] just, the other to create outward peace and prevent evil-doing." (The two governments are the "spiritual" and the "secular"). Luther, "On Secular Authority," 12.

4. Calvin, "On Civil Government," 4.20.1.

The Calvinist Roots of Evangelical Support for President Trump

An important rationale for making such a sharp distinction between these two forms of government was the propensity Calvin perceived in both the radical reformation and establishment Catholicism to conflate them. To Calvin's mind, Anabaptists subordinated the civil government to a naïve confidence in Christian perfection under the kingdom of Christ on earth, while the Catholic establishment had a tendency to reduce the kingdom of Christ to the civil government, producing "flatterers of princes" who "extol . . . their power beyond all just bounds."[5] Calvin believed that the most one could hope to witness of the kingdom of Christ during "this mortal and transitory life" was "some preludes of the heavenly kingdom" and "some prelibations of immortal and incorruptible blessedness."[6] Civil government therefore, rather than the kingdom of Christ, remains the pressing political concern for Christians.

According to Calvin, civil government represents a divine order established and upheld by God. Its purpose is to "cherish and support the external worship of God," "preserve the pure doctrine of religion," "defend the constitution of the Church," "regulate our lives in a manner requisite for the society of men," "form our manners to civil justice," "promote our concord with each other," and "establish general peace and tranquility."[7] In short, civil government is about piety, peace, and justice. Undergirding this conception of government was Calvin's keen perception of the threat posed by sin to human coexistence:

> For since the insolence of the wicked is so great, and their iniquity so obstinate, that it can scarcely be restrained by all the severity of the laws, what may we expect they would do if they found themselves at liberty to perpetuate crimes with impunity whose outrages even the arm of power cannot altogether prevent?[8]

---

5. Calvin, "On Civil Government," 4.20.1.
6. Calvin, "On Civil Government," 4.20.2.
7. Calvin, "On Civil Government," 4.20.2.
8. Calvin, "On Civil Government," 4.20.2.

The idea that human depravity justifies the existence of political order and the exercise of political authority has deep roots in Protestant political thought. Paul Ramsey, for instance, argued in *Basic Christian Ethics* that "in relations among men in larger groups, political democracy may be given compelling justification only if some reference be made to the problem of restraining and remedying sin."[9] Calvin understood Christian piety to be integral to the establishment of social peace and justice. Indeed, he elevated Christian piety to the highest end of government: "no government can be happily constituted unless its first object be the promotion of piety."[10]

In keeping with the prevailing Christian attitudes of his day, and drawing on a well-established Catholic exegetical tradition retained by magisterial reformers, Calvin believed that the Bible teaches that civil magistrates "are invested with [God's] authority and are altogether his representatives, and act as his vicegerents."[11] Ideally, rulers duly vested with God's authority ought to reflect the image of the creator in their rule: "it behooves them to watch with all care, earnestness, and diligence, that in their administration they may exhibit to men an image . . . of the providence, care, goodness, benevolence, and justice of God."[12] The qualities befitting a Christian magistrate include, according to Calvin, "an ardent pursuit of integrity, prudence, clemency, moderation, and innocence."[13]

However, Calvin thought all magistrates, irrespective of character, were owed obedience, respect, and honor by dint of the divine origin of their appointment and the divine authority vested in their office:

> A man of the worst character, and most undeserving of all honor, who holds the sovereign power, really possesses that eminent and Divine authority which the Lord

---

9. Ramsey, *Basic Christian Ethics*, 330.
10. Calvin, "On Civil Government," 4.20.9.
11. Calvin, "On Civil Government," 4.20.4.
12. Calvin, "On Civil Government," 4.20.6.
13. Calvin, "On Civil Government," 4.20.6.

> has given by his word to the ministers of his justice and judgment; and, therefore ... he ought to be regarded by his subjects, as far as pertains to public obedience, with the same reverence and esteem which they would show to the best of kings, if such a one were granted to them.[14]

This idea stems in part from a distinction Calvin made between the dignity of the office of magistrate and the character of its occupant:

> I am not speaking of the persons as if the mask of dignity ought to palliate or excuse folly, ignorance, or cruelty, and conduct the most nefarious and flagitious, and so to acquire for vices the praise due to virtues; but I affirm that the station itself is worthy of honor and reverence, so that, whoever our governors are, they ought to possess our esteem and veneration on account of the office which they fill.[15]

It also stems from the notion that God at times exercises his wrath against nations and peoples through their rulers for the purposes of punishment or edification: "for sometimes he raises up some of his servants as public avengers."[16] Calvin offered but one caveat to this general rule of obedience. In the event that a ruler commands something against God, the Christian subject is not obligated to comply in respect of that particular command.[17]

On the basis of this foray into Calvin's political theology one can readily see how a contemporary evangelical might construe their support for Trump as finding support in Calvin's political theology. An evangelical might point to Trump's nomination of Neil Gorsuch for the Supreme Court, for instance, with his strong record of defending religious rights, along with Trump's executive order promoting free speech and religious liberty,[18] as evidence that Trump is, in some sense and to some extent, promoting Christian piety in America. A critic, of course, might counter that

14. Calvin, "On Civil Government," 4.20.25.
15. Calvin, "On Civil Government," 4.20.22.
16. Calvin, "On Civil Government," 4.20.30.
17. Calvin, "On Civil Government," 4.20.32.
18. Whitehouse.gov, "Presidential Executive Order."

these actions fall far short of what Calvin understood as Christian piety and the civil government's role in promoting it. But evangelicals could retort that in the context of the United States, where the presidential choice in 2016 was binary, they backed the candidate most likely to promote Christian piety as they conceive it.

Many evangelicals evidently feel that Trump has already vindicated their support. It also bears consideration that many evangelicals feared, rightly or wrongly, that a Clinton presidency would have led to the regression of Christian piety in America and greater repression of religious freedom, thus presenting them with a clear and unambiguous choice in 2016. Evangelicals might further point to Trump's stance on Islam and immigration, again rightly or wrongly, as promoting peace and stability in America. Moreover, they might point to Gorsuch (and Kavanaugh) as evidence that Trump is fulfilling his duty to promote justice. The point is this: within the relative possibilities and constraints of the contemporary American political context, an evangelical might form the view that Trump is fulfilling the divine mandate of government, on a Calvinist interpretation, to an extent that warrants their ongoing support.

That said, the available evidence inexorably leads one to the conclusion that Trump falls well short of the ideal character of a Christian magistrate as envisioned by Calvin. While Calvin ultimately recommends submission to magistrates of poor character, he does not instruct silence with regard to poor character, nor its celebration. The extent to which Trump's evangelical supporters have achieved an appropriate balance, within a Calvinist framework, between esteem for the office of president and reprobation of the character of the occupant is an open question. In any event, while Trump *ought* to reflect the image of God, particularly as one who professes a Christian faith, the character flaws he manifests in both his personal and public life do not disqualify him from exercising God's authority, according to Calvin's understanding of civil government.

Notwithstanding the shrillest rhetoric of Trump's critics, he is no Nebuchadnezzar, the quintessential tyrant Calvin cited as evidence that God raises up servants to exact his wrath. Trump no doubt looks more like a David to evangelical supporters given his sympathetic disposition towards evangelical concerns about Christian piety and the Christian character of America. But given even a Nebuchadnezzar can exercise God's authority, it is not difficult to see how an evangelical influenced by Calvin could bring him or herself to support a latter-day David.

One of the hallmarks of Calvin's political theology that seems to find resonance in contemporary American evangelical political theology is a type of pragmatic political realism. The sharp distinction Calvin draws between the heavenly kingdom of Christ and the earthly civil government, his belief that the primary purpose of government is to restrain and remedy human wickedness, and his understanding that sometimes God exercises his authority through oppression, leaves little room for the type of utopianism often on display in other parts of the Christian theopolitical tradition, not to mention a host of secular political philosophies.[19]

Calvin firmly believes that humanity's fallen nature defers perfection until the future reign of Christ. As a corollary, it also necessitates certain compromises during our earthly pilgrimage on the way to "our true country."[20] This helps to explain Calvin's support for the necessary evils of capital punishment, war, and the occasional tyrant (at least in certain circumstances). When viewed through a Calvinist theopolitical lens, evangelical support for Trump begins to look less like a pact with the Devil and more like a prudent and pragmatic choice consistent with the divine ends of government, within the constraints of the American political context.

---

19. By the same token, it would seem to leave the North Korean Christian with nowhere to go other than to accept that the Kim dynasty has been put in place by God to punish the long-suffering people of North Korea.

20. Calvin, "On Civil Government," 4.20.2. Calvin is channelling Augustine here.

9

Christianity and the American Conservative Movement[1]

IS CONSERVATISM THE NATURAL political home of Christianity? That certainly appears to be the case if the voting habits of American Christians are anything to go by. Pew Research Center analysis indicates that 74–81 percent of white, born-again, evangelical Christians and 52–60 percent of white Catholics have voted for the Republican candidate in each of the last four presidential elections.[2] In the 2016 presidential race, regular churchgoers voted 56 percent Trump to 40 percent Clinton, while the religiously unaffiliated voted 68 percent Clinton to 26 percent Trump.[3]

Individuals vote for a host of different reasons, in which case it is difficult to generalize about what drove Christian support for Trump. The one certainty is that motivations will vary. Irrespective of the reasons behind Christian support for Trump and the Republican Party, conservatism appears to resonate with more

---

1. Originally published as "Conservatives' Core Values Not as Theologically Grounded as Many Believe," *The Political Theology Network*.

2. Smith and Martínez, "How the Faithful Voted." At the 100-day mark of Trump's presidency, 78 percent of "white evangelical protestants" approved of Trump, 64 percent "very strongly." Smith, "Among White Evangelicals."

3. Smith and Martínez, "How the Faithful Voted."

Christians in America than liberalism does. That resonance forms the subject of the present chapter. In particular, I wish to interrogate the extent to which core conservative values appear to be grounded in or supported by Christian theology. The conservative values discussed below have been drawn from a survey of the vision and mission statements of prominent conservative political organizations in the United States. These include: The Heritage Foundation, The American Conservative Union, Citizens United, Americans for Constitutional Liberty (The Conservative Caucus), Eagle Forum, Family Research Council, FreedomWorks, and the John Birch Society. I have also considered the preamble of the "Republican Platform 2016." Suffice to say, there is far more to the conservative movement than the mission statements of prominent think tanks and lobbying organizations. A more comprehensive and systematic analysis would necessarily take account of the intellectual origins of the conservative movement found in the influential work of William F. Buckley and Russell Kirk, both of whom were practicing Catholics. Still, the values investigated here were held, to one extent or another, as core conservative values by both Buckley and Kirk, even if they might not agree with their exact formulation in the current political context.

The mission statements of the aforementioned self-described conservative political organizations reveal an impressively consistent set of principles and values that can be taken as representative of political conservatism in the United States. They include: "free enterprise," "limited government," "individual freedom," "traditional American values," "national sovereignty," and "strong families." There are further discrete positions and interests expressed in the mission statements, but these generally fit within the purview of one or another of the principles or values stated above. For example, the notion of limited taxation can be said to fall within the scope of "limited government." Similarly, educational freedom falls within the scope of "individual freedom," opposition to same-sex marriage within "strong families," and support for a "strong defense" within "national sovereignty."

The question I pose is this: what theological grounds, if any, support these principles? I pose this question from a deliberately agnostic position as to the relative merits of the values and principles themselves. The foundational concept that appears to bind together the principles of the kind of conservativism represented by our sample organizations is "freedom" (also "liberty"). The importance of "free enterprise," for example, is often explained by its relationship to "individual freedoms." The preamble to the 2016 Republican platform states that "political freedom and economic freedom are indivisible."[4] "Limited government" is similarly linked to the preservation of individual freedoms—its primary purpose is to restrict the ability of government to interfere with or curb individual freedoms. According to the American Conservative Union, "capitalism is the only economic system of our time that is compatible with political liberty" and "liberties can remain secure only if government is so limited that it cannot infringe upon [a citizen's inherent] rights."[5]

The defining characteristic of conservatism—at least in its contemporary American guise—thus appears to be individual freedom. This helps to sharpen the focus of the question posed above, such that we are really seeking the theological grounds for conservatism's politics of individual freedom. Although conservative values and principles are generally not supported explicitly with theological arguments (at least not in mission statements), one important theological theme does recur. This is the notion that God has endowed humans with inalienable rights, which by implication require certain political and economic freedoms in order to flourish and to be preserved. The American Conservative Union, for instance, maintains that "our inherent rights are endowed by the Creator" and maintains that "God is the author of life, liberty, and the family."[6] The notion of inalienable rights

---

4. American Presidency Project, "2016 Republican Party Platform."

5. American Conservative Union, "What We Believe."

6. American Conservative Union, "What We Believe"; Family Research Council, "FAQs."

obviously has a long, if somewhat uneven, pedigree in the United States, going back to its very political foundation.

The notion of God-given inalienable political rights provides an entry point into a discussion of the theological grounds for contemporary American conservatism. The theology of conservatism appears to rely substantially on a doctrine of creation. There are two arms to this theological support. The first is anthropological. It holds that humans are, by their nature, autonomous creatures with free will and an inherent desire and need for social environments that facilitate and protect the expression of that free will. The second is an *imago Dei* argument. If humans owe their nature to God, their creator, then their inherent autonomy and commensurate desire and need for freedom must be God-given. This creationist account of freedom serves as more than mere explanation for the existence of individual rights. It lends theological authority to the notion that individual freedom is something that the Christian in good conscience can fight for and defend in the political arena.

It is interesting to note that the sacred text most frequently cited in support of conservatism's creation principles and values is not the Bible, but the American Declaration of Independence and the American Constitution. The latter is described in the preamble to the "Republican Platform 2016" as "our enduring covenant."[7] This is not to say that the concept of freedom is absent from the Bible. The biblical authors clearly had the conceptual and social categories of freedom and slavery. But the Bible's primary interest appears to be freedom from sin, not social or political emancipation, notwithstanding the profound influence of emancipationist political theologies in the second half of the twentieth century, including the civil rights movement in the US and liberation theology in Latin America. John 8:31–35 provides an interesting example of the "freedom from sin" motif in relation to the sociology of slavery:

> Then Jesus said to the Jews who had believed in him, "If you continue in my word, you are truly my disciples; and you will know the truth, and the truth will make you

7. American Presidency Project, "2016 Republican Party Platform."

free." They answered him, "We are descendants of Abraham and have never been slaves to anyone. What do you mean by saying, "You will be made free?" Jesus answered them, "Very truly, I tell you, everyone who commits sin is a slave to sin. The slave does not have a permanent place in the household; the son has a place there forever. So if the Son makes you free, you will be free indeed.

Jesus preached freedom from slavery to sin. Does it follow then that Jesus also stood for individual rights, free enterprise, limited government, national sovereignty, and traditional American values? It is impossible to say, as these are all modern concepts unfamiliar in Jesus' day. Are such values therefore *un*-Christian? No. It just means that the Bible is silent on core issues that preoccupy the modern conservative movement. The Bible does not offer, for example, an economic theory—market-based or otherwise. Nor does it take a position on the size and role of government. Furthermore, it is silent on many of the more discrete positions expressed by the contemporary conservative movement in the United States such as the right to homeschool, limited taxation, the right to bear arms, and a strong national defense.

The fact that the Bible does not offer anything resembling the nature and content of the "Republican Platform 2016" does not gainsay the theological basis of conservatism's foundational concept "freedom." It is difficult to deny that humans are born with an innate capacity and desire for freedom. For the Christian who believes God created man and woman in his image, it seems entirely reasonable, if not necessary, to attribute human freedom to *imago Dei*. It is equally undeniable that the attenuation or outright suppression of freedom does great harm to human well-being at both the personal and societal level. No one of sound mind aspires to become their neighbor's slave. We all instinctively crave personal freedom and instinctively react negatively to its infringement. Freedom is thus a personal, social, and political good worth fighting for, as many peoples have done throughout the ages, including in America.

Christianity and the American Conservative Movement

But if we accept that individual freedom is part of *imago Dei*, does it follow that free enterprise, limited government, traditional American values, and national sovereignty reflect God's image? Do these values form part of the created order? The truth is that they are not actually theological concepts. They are the product of rational philosophical reflection, experience, and human ingenuity.[8] In other words, they cannot be construed as revealed truths, at least not in Christianity's revelatory texts.

The observation that these principles are grounded in philosophical reasoning rather than revelation does not imply their illegitimacy. It merely clarifies the nature of many core conservative principles and values and their relationship to Christian theology. If the characteristic values of contemporary conservatism in America are philosophically grounded rather than theologically grounded, notwithstanding the movement's theologically grounded (in the doctrine of creation) foundational concept of God-given individual freedom, then the question remains: why do the majority of American Christians habitually vote Republican? Is it because a majority of Christians are persuaded by the philosophical cogency of conservatism? Or, is it possible that some, perhaps many, overestimate the theological basis of the contemporary American conservative movement? Political ideologies and philosophies are routinely sacralized across the left–right spectrum, and it is possible that some (perhaps many) Christian conservatives in America have succumbed to this temptation. But the possible false-sacralization of the conservative movement in America does not preclude Christians embracing a conservative political philosophy—this can conceivably be done on sound philosophical grounds alone.

There is, of course, another possibility. Some Christians who vote conservative might do so on account of specific issues rather than the larger philosophical framework of conservatism per se. There are plentiful issues of special concern to Christian voters, such as abortion, Supreme Court appointments, the right

---

8. Cavanaugh describes politics as "a practice of the imagination." Cavanaugh, *Theopolitical Imagination*, 1.

to educate children according to one's religious convictions, and religious liberty. These issues tend to find greater support in the Republican Party than the Democratic Party. Hence issue-motivated Christian voters might choose the Republican Party on the basis of single issues and without necessarily embracing the entire conservative political agenda.

There is one part of the conservative values-system that is more difficult to reconcile with the foundational concept of individual freedom. This is "strong families." The notion of "strong families," like "individual freedom," can also claim theological foundation, for it is an issue upon which the Bible does have something to say. The Bible, and with it the church (at least traditionally), has a specific view of marriage and sexual relations. While Christians can and do take different positions on the question of same-sex marriage, there is no dispute that those Christians who uphold a "traditional" view of marriage overwhelmingly do so on theological grounds. It is possible therefore that some, perhaps many, Christian conservatives are conservative first and foremost on account of their support for a particular *Christian* view of the family and its pivotal role in society, rather than, say, a passion for the unbridled right to accumulate private wealth. However, the conservative (traditional) Christian view of the family arguably cuts against the very grain of individual freedom. The question of same-sex marriage, for instance, has proven to be a point of tension between right-leaning libertarians and conservatives, with many in the former camp supporting same-sex marriage on the basis of the paramountcy of individual freedom.

While conservatism is premised on a foundational concept that Christians can genuinely support on theological grounds—our created freedom—and supports a theologically-rooted view of the family that these days is universally regarded as conservative, the reality is that some of its most cherished values do not appear to be theologically-grounded, at least not in any obvious or unambiguous way. This is not to say that they are therefore incompatible with Christian theology or cannot be supported in good conscience by Christians. It simply means that conservatism is a political philosophy, not Christian revelation or theological doctrine, in which case the rationale for Christians embracing its full agenda will unavoidably rely to some extent on philosophical reasoning.

This helps to highlight two attitudes that the politically conservative Christian ought to bring to their politics. The first is to avoid sacralizing conservatism. It is unnecessary. Conservatism is a secular political philosophy. This is why atheists are able to embrace it with the same enthusiasm, if not always for exactly the same reasons, as Christians do. Indeed, Russell Kirk, one of the conservative movement's foremost figures, was not a Christian at the time he penned one of the movement's seminal texts, *The Conservative Mind*.[9] The politically conservative Christian can argue that conservatism is compatible with the Bible and Christian theology, that it reflects *some* aspects of Christian teaching, or that *certain* Christian principles form part of the philosophy. A Christian could even argue that conservatism *best* reflects the spirit, ethos, and teaching of Christianity. What is more difficult to argue is that conservatism self-evidently represents the *only* biblically- or theologically-grounded political *theology*. The second attitude is thus a disposition of epistemic humility in recognition that the Christian conservative, like many of their Christian political opponents, strives to live a life obedient to God in a fallen world, in which even the best political minds are liable to illusion and delusion.

---

9. Kirk grew up in an irreligious family and was only received into the Catholic Church in 1964, eleven years after he published *The Conservative Mind* in 1953, although the "rather slow and complex process" by which he came to Christian faith began several years after its publication. Kirk, *Sword of Imagination*, 231–33.

10

The Politics of Jesus and Christian Anarchism

Reading Yoder and Ellul in the Trump Apocalypse[1]

INTRODUCTION

TRUMP'S HEADY TENURE AS CEO of America Inc. has eviscerated political orthodoxy with insouciant aplomb. Shareholders remain split, with displays of rapturous ecstasy and apocalyptic terror at either end of the political spectrum. Much intellectual energy has understandably been expended on analysis of what the enduring impact of the age of Trump will mean for the Republican Party and conservatism in the longer term, in light of Trump's hostile takeover of the party to enfeebled cries of heresy by conservative dissenters. There is little doubt that the GOP and the conservative movement more broadly will be transformed by what looks set to be a pivotal moment in American political history. But as Einstein proverbially put it, "for every action, there is an equal and opposite

---

1. Originally published as "John Howard Yoder and the New Prospects for a Christian Politics," *The Political Theology Network*.

reaction." To that end the Trump era will not only be marked by transformations on the right, but equal and opposite transformations on the left. For the Democratic Party and progressive politics will not emerge from the Trump experience unaltered.

The Trump moment represents a challenge for Christians on the left, who have traditionally adhered to pacifism in one form or another. For there is the risk that the ying to Trump's yang will include one of the left's enduring pathologies: violent protest, disruption, and disorder. This has already been in evidence in the emergence of Antifa, the assault of Trump supporters, and riotous behavior on university campuses in response to the appearance of conservative speakers. A perennial challenge for the Christian left has been to forge a distinctive, authentic progressive Christian political vision that amounts to more than a slavish imitation of popular secular ideological fashions, and that avoids contamination by the most extreme expressions of those fashions (there is an equal and opposite risk on the Christian right).

In this chapter I critically examine the political theology of two prominent Christian thinkers who could reasonably be regarded as sitting on the left hand of the conventional left–right political spectrum: American Mennonite theologian John Howard Yoder (1927–1997) and French Reformed philosopher Jacques Ellul (1912–1994).

JOHN HOWARD YODER'S "REVOLUTIONARY SUBORDINATION"

Yoder's highly influential 1972 book *The Politics of Jesus* advances the thesis that "Jesus is, according to the biblical witness, a model of radical political action."[2] In order to appreciate the impact of *The Politics of Jesus* it is important to understand the context in which it was written. Yoder sought to counter the then-prevailing narrative that Jesus was not relevant to "questions of social ethics" and that his life and teaching purely touched the spiritual domain rather

2. Yoder, *Politics of Jesus*, 2.

than the political.³ In this effort he largely succeeded. Indeed, *The Politics of Jesus* retains an enduring influence in political theology to this day. The political "model" Yoder discerned in Jesus' life and teaching was something he called "revolutionary subordination." As he explained, Jesus'

> motto of revolutionary subordination, of willing servanthood in the place of domination, enables the person in a subordinate position in society to accept and live within that status without resentment . . . The subordinate person becomes a free ethical agent in the act of voluntarily acceding to subordination in the power of Christ instead of bowing to it either fatalistically or resentfully.⁴

Jesus' "revolutionary subordination" was exemplified, according to Yoder, in the way that he submitted freely and innocently to the injustice of death by crucifixion at the hands of the Jewish and Roman authorities in first-century Palestine. Yoder maintained that

> there is thus but one realm in which the concept of imitation holds . . . [and] this is at the point of the concrete social meaning of the cross in its relation to enmity and power. Servanthood replaces dominion, forgiveness absorbs hostility.⁵

Yoder believed (with some scriptural warrant) that present reality is characterized by two coexisting "ages" or "aeons."⁶ The coming aeon is the aeon of "redemptive reality," while the present aeon is a realm of sin. In fact, there is "a very strong strand of Gospel teaching," according to Yoder, which portrays secular government as "the province of the sovereignty of Satan."⁷ This places politics and the church into irreconcilable opposition, with the church assuming "absolute priority . . . over the state in the plan of God."⁸ It

---

3. Yoder, *Politics of Jesus*, 5.
4. Yoder, *Politics of Jesus*, 186.
5. Yoder, *Politics of Jesus*, 131.
6. Yoder, *Christian Witness to the State*, 9.
7. Yoder, *Politics of Jesus*, 194.
8. Yoder, *Christian Witness to the State*, 17.

The Politics of Jesus and Christian Anarchism

is this negative view of the legitimacy of political authority in the present aeon that places Yoder's political authority into the orbit of the left, arguably the far left.

The way Yoder handles Rom 13:1–7, traditionally cited to uphold the legitimacy of governing authorities, is instructive. On Yoder's reading God merely "orders" the powers that be. He neither blesses nor ordains them. Nor does he create or institute them. What God does is keep political authorities in their place. As far as Yoder is concerned, the fact that God "orders" secular governments reveals nothing about how they ought to be organized.[9] The moral injunction in Rom 13:1–7 is for Christians to eschew "any notion of revolution or insubordination," a temptation arising from the illegitimacy of political authority. The Christian call is to adopt a "nonresistant attitude toward a tyrannical government" in the form of "revolutionary subordination."[10]

Yoder offers several concrete examples of what he envisages in connection with "revolutionary subordination":

> Subordination is significantly different from obedience. The conscientious objector who refuses to do what government demands, but still remains under the sovereignty of that government and accepts the penalties which it imposes, or the Christian who refuses to worship Caesar but still permits Caesar to put him or her to death, is being subordinate even though not obeying.[11]

Yoder does not preach mere passivity vis-à-vis political authority. Political authority is to be radically, albeit nonviolently, resisted, for at base it is illegitimate and carries no intrinsic authority of its own. Secular political authority is essentially a form of demonic power. That power is ordered by God as a means of mediating man's rebellion and the coming age of redemption. Subordination therefore draws its authority from God's command and Christ's model, which Christians are to follow dutifully.

---

9. Yoder, *Politics of Jesus*, 202.
10. Yoder, *Politics of Jesus*, 202.
11. Yoder, *Politics of Jesus*, 209.

JACQUES ELLUL'S "CHRISTIAN ANARCHISM"

Ellul, like Yoder, developed a "politics of Jesus" that was hostile to the notion of legitimate political authority. Indeed, he went further than Yoder's "revolutionary subordination" to argue that "Christian anarchism" is the political stance modeled by Jesus ("anarchy" in the sense of no authority or domination, not in the sense of "disorder"[12]). As he explained in the aptly titled *Anarchy and Christianity*,

> the more I studied and the more I understood seriously the biblical message in its entirety . . . the more I came to see how impossible it is to give simple obedience to the state and how there is in the Bible the orientation to a certain anarchism.[13]

Ellul conceded that the Bible does contain "texts which seem to validate authority."[14] But he maintained that it is possible to identify a "general current" in the Bible "which points toward anarchy."[15] Ellul adopted a two-pronged hermeneutic strategy to substantiate his anarchist reading of the Bible. The first consisted of identifying an anti-statist attitude in Israel. Ellul understood the kings of Israel to be equivalent to the state in the modern era. Israel's anti-royalist sentiment could therefore be equated to an anti-statist sentiment more broadly.[16] In support of Israel's anti-statism, Ellul pointed to the fact that "in the biblical account "good" kings are always defeated by Israel's enemies, and the "great" kings who win victories and extend their borders are always "bad.""[17] He further highlighted the political situation portrayed in the book of Judges: "in those days there was no king in Israel; all the people did what was right in their own eyes" (Judg 21:25).[18] Finally, he pointed to

---

12. Ellul, *Anarchy and Christianity*, 45.
13. Ellul, *Anarchy and Christianity*, 3.
14. Ellul, *Anarchy and Christianity*, 46.
15. Ellul, *Anarchy and Christianity*, 46.
16. Ellul, *Anarchy and Christianity*, 52.
17. Ellul, *Anarchy and Christianity*, 50.
18. Ellul, *Anarchy and Christianity*, 47.

the prophetic critique of Israel's kings—"their writings, usually in opposition to power, were preserved, were regarded as a revelation of God, and were listened to by the people."[19]

The second prong consisted of identifying the same anti-statist sentiment in the life and teaching of Jesus, whose "attitude," according to Ellul, "was one of total rejection and scorn for all religious or political authority."[20] Jesus treated political power "with disdain and did not accord it any authority."[21] The reason, as for Yoder, is that political authority "belongs to the devil."[22] Thus, in sympathy with Yoder, Ellul regards Jesus' submission to the injustice of Roman political authority as an act of radical political defiance:

> The fact that Jesus submits to the trial is not in these circumstances a recognition of the legitimacy of the authority of government. On the contrary, it is an unveiling of the basic injustice of what purports to be justice . . . We thus find here once again the conviction of the biblical writers that all authority is unjust.[23]

The proper attitude of the Christian, then, just as it was for Yoder, is a defiant refusal to recognize the legitimacy of political authority.

DID JESUS HAVE A POLITICS?

Yoder's "revolutionary subordination" and Ellul's "Christian anarchism" are contentious. The heart of that contention stems from the notion that Jesus represents a *model* of political action, radical or otherwise. It is one thing to argue that Jesus' life and teaching is relevant and instructive for the development of a Christian political theology. It is another thing entirely to argue that Jesus offers

---

19. Ellul, *Anarchy and Christianity*, 51.
20. Ellul, *Anarchy and Christianity*, 67–68.
21. Ellul, *Anarchy and Christianity*, 56.
22. Ellul, *Anarchy and Christianity*, 58.
23. Ellul, *Anarchy and Christianity*, 66–67.

a normative political "model" that the Christian can, or ought, to follow.

The problem relates to the Bible's lack of explicit articulation in favor of Yoder's "revolutionary subordination" or Ellul's anarchist "current." The fact of the matter is that Jesus had very little to say explicitly about politics, as did those who wrote about him. Collectively, they demonstrate no great interest in political theory per se and do not even appear to have been particularly preoccupied with practical political questions. This probably goes some way to explaining why it is that Christianity has managed to inspire everything from Ellul's Christian anarchism to theocratic monarchism (the dominant political model of the church throughout much of its history).[24]

The crux of the problem, then, is that Yoder's and Ellul's political models are their own extrapolations from the life and teaching of Jesus. It is eminently possible that these models might come as a surprise to the biblical authors from whom they are purportedly derived. The fact that "revolutionary subordination" and "Christian anarchism" are models that Yoder and Ellul extrapolate or infer from their own reading of the New Testament does not, in and of itself, invalidate the models. Extrapolation and inference are, after all, unavoidable hazards of the theologian's trade, particularly the political theologian's. It does, however, seem to call for a high burden of proof, higher than that offered by either Yoder or Ellul. That burden is for both to cogently demonstrate that their model is the only clear and unambiguous political model that can be inferred from the entire narrative structure and content of the Bible. The fact that a majority of Christians, both past and present, have drawn the obverse conclusion regarding political authority, i.e., that it is legitimate and serves God's purposes, suggests that the models advocated by Yoder and Ellul are not so clearly and unambiguously to be found in the Bible.[25]

24. Kuyper was of the view that "God's own direct government is absolutely *monarchial*," and that this mode of divine government characterized both the prelapsarian and post-eschatological state of humankind. Kuyper, *Lectures on Calvinism*, 83. Emphasis original.

25. Dooyeweerd, for example, believed that the state is a "genuinely

The Politics of Jesus and Christian Anarchism

The real problem might simply be the very idea that Jesus represents a political model at all. If it is to be supposed that Jesus revealed a normative political model of action in the way he lived his earthly life, wouldn't he conceivably have said as much, or at least included clearer and more explicit teaching in that regard? Wouldn't Paul have addressed it more extensively than the seven verses in chapter 13 of his epistle to the church at Rome? Moreover, why did the Christian tradition develop a doctrine of *imitatio Christi* from its reading of the Scriptures but not Yoder's and Ellul's *imitatio Christi politici*?

It is not difficult to discern a reason why the pre- and post-Constantinian church did not develop a doctrine of *imitatio Christi politici* along the lines of either "revolutionary subordination" or "Christian anarchism." Christian tradition arrived at an understanding of the meaning and purpose of Jesus' life and teaching through the framework of salvation, not political activism. As John's Gospel succinctly puts it: "For God so loved the world that he gave his only Son, so that everyone who believes in him may not perish but may have eternal life (3:16)." Christian traditions differ over precisely how Jesus' atoning sacrifice works itself out in practice, but they have never lost sight of the fact that the central meaning and purpose of Jesus' life and teaching was salvation. That much is agreed. Furthermore, the early church also arrived at a view of politics that regarded secular political authority as not only legitimate, but God-given. This view predates the Constantinian revolution.[26] It is therefore difficult to discern the precise basis upon which Yoder and Ellul believe Christ's salvific

---

Christian idea . . . rooted in the radical, Scriptural view regarding the relationship between the Kingdom of God in Christ Jesus and the temporal societal structures." Dooyeweerd, *Christian Idea of the State*, 4. Offering yet another perspective, Schmemann avers that "the power of the Cross—the Church's essential weapon against the demons—liberated the empire from the power of the "prince of this world" . . . [making] the empire "open" to the Kingdom, available as its servant and instrument," albeit without "transform[ing] the empire *into* the Kingdom of God." Schmemann, *Church, World, Mission*, 36. Emphasis original.

26. See, for example, *First Clement*, 61.1 and *The Martyrdom of Polycarp*, 10.2, thought to have been written in the first and second centuries respectively.

mission *also* reveals the normative political model for Christians. This of course does not gainsay the political significance of Jesus' life. Even if one privileges salvation as the prism through which to understand Jesus' life, that life still has significant implication for politics, including political authority. But thinking through the political implications of Jesus' life is of a rather different order from discerning and following the purported political model represented by that life.

A particular weakness of Yoder's argument, it seems to me, is that it does not sufficiently take into account the very profound ontological distinction between the model, i.e., the *theanthropos* Jesus, and those meant to emulate him, i.e., finite and fallen humans. Yoder sees the cross as the pinnacle of Jesus' radical political action and the embodiment of "revolutionary subordination." But even if we accept this, in what sense can it really be construed as an analogy for human political action? Jesus' life culminated in his death, resurrection, ascension, *and rule* at the right hand of the Father. Yet "revolutionary subordination" lays its foundation in Jesus' death, not his resurrection or exaltation, let alone his kingship. It is not difficult to see why. Sacrificial death is an aspect of Jesus' life that humans *can* emulate, if not always literally, then at least in spirit. Rising from the dead, ascending to heaven and ruling at the right hand of the father, and releasing humankind from the bonds of sin, on the other hand, are not. The point is that we are not heirs to the Davidic throne or Sons of Man, in which case there are important aspects of Jesus' life that do not offer a political model for humans. The fact that the purported politics of Jesus is derived from some aspects of Jesus' life, but not others, renders the whole scheme arbitrary.[27]

CONCLUSION

What can Yoder's "revolutionary subordination" and Ellul's "Christian anarchism" constructively offer the secular left in its current

27. This is perhaps a criticism that could be leveled against all Christian political theology.

moment of paroxysm? Yoder and Ellul appear to share the far-left view that political authority is illegitimate, thus providing a unique basis for dialogue between Christians upholding a political theology inspired by Yoder or Ellul and today's radicals. What Yoder and Ellul have to offer latter-day leftist warriors tempted by violence is an alternative model of response to political authority, especially when it is abused. That response is nonviolent resistance. Yoder in particular understood the virtue of political order, notwithstanding the illegitimacy of political authority as he understood it. God puts political authority into some kind of order so that humans can live in harmony. This important distinction between the social good of political order, on the one hand, and the illegitimacy of particular political authorities, on the other, could potentially offer the radical left a means of restricting their ire to the current occupant of the White House rather than the entire institutional order upon which theirs and all of our well-being depends.

11

Political Anthropology and the Post-Liberal Future[1]

LIBERALISM IS MANIFESTLY IN the throes of a profound crisis of legitimacy. It feels like only yesterday that the liberal world order was able to nonchalantly bask in its triumphant "end of history."[2] Yet today, even the prophet of that triumph fears for democracy's future.[3] The political tumult of Brexit and Trumpism has seen the erstwhile faithful question the orthodoxy of liberal dogma. In fact, serious intellectuals can now seriously countenance the idea of a benign, or indeed improved, post-liberal future for humanity *and* find an audience that will read them seriously.

A seminal contribution to post-liberal rumination is John Milbank and Adrian Pabst's *The Politics of Virtue: Post-Liberalism and the Human Future*. *The Politics of Virtue* offers a withering and sobering critique of the "metacrises" besetting liberal politics, economy, polity, and culture. The book's fundamental claim is that "liberalism as a philosophy and an ideology turns out to be contradictory, self-defeating, and parasitic on the legacy of

1. Originally published as "Political Anthropology and the Post-Liberal Future, *The Political Theology Network*.
2. See Fukuyama, *End of History*.
3. Tharoor, "The man who declared the 'end of history.'"

Greco-Roman civilization and the Judeo-Christian tradition."[4] Its chief insight is that the "social-cultural liberalism" of the left and the "economic-political liberalism" of the right have conspired to form a vapid centrist consensus committed to "limitless liberalization and mindless modernization."[5] For Milbank and Pabst, this unholy alliance represents the "victory of vice over virtue" and has bequeathed societies committed to "selfishness, greed, suspicion, and coercion over common benefit, generosity, a measure of trust, and persuasive power."[6]

One may quibble here and there with the diagnostics, but Milbank and Pabst serve as compelling witnesses to the poor health of liberalism. The fundamental question, however, is whether the patient is ill or dying. Milbank and Pabst suggest the latter, recommending a post-liberal alternative to liberalism cast as the "politics of virtue." The politics of virtue "seeks to fuse greater economic justice with social reciprocity," "proposes gift-exchange or social reciprocity as the ultimate principle to govern *both* the economic and the political realms," and "propose[s] a reciprocalist model of sharing risk, responsibilities, and resources wherein reward is reconnected to personal requirements both for varied self-fulfillment and for rendering a social contribution."[7]

There is much to admire in these and similar proposals that form part of Milbank and Pabst's post-liberal vision. However, as Oliver O'Donovan once observed, "large moral disagreements all turn on competing descriptions," in which case "serious moral debate cannot avoid arbitrating questions of description and so enquiring into the structures of reality."[8] It is the "structure of reality" underpinning Milbank and Pabst's critique of liberalism's metacrises that I wish to probe in this chapter. For the descriptive realism of the book's account of liberalism is determinative of the cogency of its proposed post-liberal alternative.

4. Milbank and Pabst, *Politics of Virtue*, 2.
5. Milbank and Pabst, *Politics of Virtue*, 1, 13.
6. Milbank and Pabst, *Politics of Virtue*, 2. "Liberalism" in this context denotes classical liberalism.
7. Milbank and Pabst, *Politics of Virtue*, 3. Emphasis original.
8. O'Donovan, *Desire of the Nations*, 14.

Milbank and Pabst provocatively claim that the structural reality of liberalism is "voluntary servitude and obsequiousness."[9] These are presented as the ineluctable ends of certain constitutive characteristics of liberalism, namely individualism, negative liberty, and anthropological pessimism. Milbank and Pabst insist that liberalism and post-liberalism are qualitatively different and fundamentally incompatible. Take the issue of liberalism's negative liberty, defined by Milbank and Pabst as "unfettered personal choice and freedom from constraint except the law and private conscience."[10] Our authors want to see negative liberty replaced with the post-liberal virtue of "positive liberty," defined as "the self-release of people from debilitating passions and degrading choices, in favor of the more strenuous pursuit of human flourishing."[11] They contend that "a priority of positive freedom leaves no place for negative liberty whatsoever."[12] But are they right to insist that negative liberty precludes positive liberty? Is it empirically compelling to claim that liberalism comprehensively negates the ability of human beings to conquer their passions and flourish? This is a verdict that will come as a surprise to many citizens of liberal societies, particularly women, racial minorities, and members of the LGBTIQ community, for many of whom the "negative liberty" of "unfettered personal choice and freedom from constraint except the law and private conscience" has facilitated rather than diminished their flourishing. No one suffers from the delusion that liberalism currently represents a bigotry-free nirvana. But on any objective measure, women and minorities have fared far better in contemporary liberal orders than in any rival, past or present.

The dichotomy Milbank and Pabst paint between negative liberty and positive liberty is indicative of a more significant underlying dichotomy between liberalism and post-liberalism that runs the course of the book. That dichotomy, in my view, is highly contentious and brings into question the descriptive realism of

9. Milbank and Pabst, *Politics of Virtue*, 19.
10. Milbank and Pabst, *Politics of Virtue*, 15.
11. Milbank and Pabst, *Politics of Virtue*, 15.
12. Milbank and Pabst, *Politics of Virtue*, 18.

the book. We are presented with a long list of post-liberal virtues (many of which I find attractive) that purportedly are required to free us from the tyranny of liberalism. They include "mutual obligation," "solidarity," "pluralist organicism," "constitutional corporatism," "personalism," and "subsidiarity."[13] But are these really all non-existent in liberal democracies? Or, more to the point, are they really only attainable by jettisoning liberalism? These virtues all exist to varying extents, albeit often imperfectly and inconsistently, in various parts of the liberal world, as indeed Milbank and Pabst concede when they point to their existence as illustrative of what is required to replace liberalism.

Upon reading *The Politics of Virtue*, one is struck by just how little structural change is actually proposed to free us from our structural imprisonment to liberalism. We are told, for instance, that we need to show more "respect for the necessity of every role" in society, that we need "an alternative business ethos . . . [that] . . . would seek to instill the pursuit of self-worth," and that civil servants need to once again "mediate between elected powers and the more continuous powers and institutions."[14] As far as I can see, proposals of this nature seem to call for cultural and attitudinal change rather than radical or even substantial structural change.

In making this observation I do not mean to suggest that such proposals are unmeritorious or that they would make no positive difference if implemented. It is just that, if liberalism and a post-liberal politics of virtue really were qualitatively different and fundamentally incompatible, then one might reasonably expect something more in the genre of the Communist Manifesto—a complete redrawing of political and economic institutions and relationships.

Moreover, one could argue that many of the proposed post-liberal virtues appear to be logically dependent on the very structural obstacles that are said to negate their possibility in the first place. In what cogent sense can it be argued that the "satisfying

---

13. Milbank and Pabst, *Politics of Virtue*, 70, 83–84, 88, 209.
14. Milbank and Pabst, *Politics of Virtue*, 73–74, 224.

and releasing of creative individuality" that is the goal of post-liberalism's "positive liberty" is not dependent on the very "negative liberty" it is supposed to replace? "Freedom of choice" might not be a sufficient condition for human flourishing, and if abused, as it all too often is in liberal societies, it undoubtedly can lead to human degeneration. But is it not a necessary condition for human flourishing? Can virtue and the good be realized by compulsion or coercion, or do they intrinsically require some degree of personal freedom, including freedom of choice? The alternative to free choice would appear to be some form of coercive paternalism whereby the state, perhaps, forces people to pursue their own good by removing their freedom to make bad choices, the latter to be determined presumably by virtuous rulers.

Interestingly, Milbank and Pabst concede that the liberal ideology of servitude has, somewhat paradoxically, produced some very welcome and profound advancements towards human flourishing, such as the aforementioned emancipation of women and minorities. But these are only paradoxes if one accepts that liberalism leads to servitude. Alternatively, we might call into question the veracity of the description of liberalism in *The Politics of Virtue* that creates the paradox in the first place.

I believe the root cause of the false dichotomy Milbank and Pabst draw between liberalism and post-liberalism stems from their political anthropology. To add to O'Donovan's maxim about competing descriptions in great moral debates, I submit that disagreements over political vision often turn on competing political anthropologies. Milbank and Pabst claim that liberalism is founded on a pessimistic Hobbesian view of human nature. "Liberal ideas and institutions," they contend, "rest on a violent ontology and a pessimistic anthropology that incentivize and reward bad behavior."[15] This pessimistic anthropology, however, turns out to be an ontological fraud, according to Milbank and Pabst. Yet, in another stroke of paradox, we are told that liberalism's fraudulent anthropology has nevertheless come to define our *actual* existence: "the supreme irony of liberal theory is that the pessimism and

15. Milbank and Pabst, *Politics of Virtue*, 3.

Political Anthropology and the Post-Liberal Future

cynicism with regard to human nature, which it falsely assumes in theory, it truly delivers in practice over time."[16] Conversely, our real, if historically latent, anthropology is said to be the natural propensity towards virtue and an inherent desire and ability to pursue the good. The post-liberal virtuous *anthropos* simply needs to be freed from the shackles of liberalism's false ontology of violence and its unduly pessimistic anthropology in order to proceed towards a more harmonious (and virtuous) destiny.

Utopian political anthropologies have a poor track record when it comes to human flourishing. Tens of millions died in the twentieth century in the misguided effort to perfect human nature. Milbank and Pabst categorically do not recommend anything akin to Stalin's great terror in the name of engineering human progress. But the question lingers: is the underlying anthropology of their post-liberal vision too optimistic to bear the weight of expectations? The great scandal of liberalism for post-liberals like Milbank and Pabst, it seems to me, is that their optimistic post-liberal political anthropology commits them to a violent view of liberalism, even though by every metric available liberal democracies are far less violent than their non-liberal contemporaries and predecessors. And yet everywhere one looks outside the liberal world one finds real structural violence. It is autocratic Syria, not liberal Great Britain, that is most proximate to Hobbes's "war of all against all." The idea that Australians, for example, are chafing under the oppression of liberalism's structural violence while entire generations of Syrians have their lives and livelihoods destroyed by a violent contest between two *illiberal* forces makes one question whether Milbank and Pabst have arrived at an accurate view of the political anthropology of liberalism. One could pose a similar question with regard to the notion that liberalism produces "servitude" in a world containing North Korea.

Milbank and Pabst's post-liberal politics of virtue seeks to retrieve and revive the best of the pre-liberal Greco-Roman and Judeo-Christian traditions. But that which is most curiously absent from *The Politics of Virtue* is the foundational anthropology

16. Milbank and Pabst, *Politics of Virtue*, 78.

of the Bible, with its emphasis on the problem of sin. The biblical narrative revolves around a good creation fallen and redeemed in Christ with the eschatological hope of a new creation. There is dispute amongst Christian traditions and theologians about how far the good creation has fallen on account of sin and how high it has risen on account of redemption. But the presence and problematic of sin is a constant across all accounts.

The Bible teaches that humans are a frustrating and paradoxical mix of good and evil. As Paul soberingly wrote, "For I do not do the good I want, but the evil I do not want is what I do (Rom 7:19)." Furthermore, this biblical anthropology finds ample support in the historical record and our own empirical experience. As G. K. Chesterton inimitably put it, sin is "a fact as practical as potatoes."[17] There is a doctrine of *liberal* sin in *The Politics of Virtue,* but no doctrine of *original* sin, as far as I can see. Milbank and Pabst may be right that liberalism's anthropology is too pessimistic. But I confess to finding the anthropology of *The Politics of Virtue* balanced too far in the opposite direction.

My criticism is not that Milbank and Pabst have mistaken an angel for the devil. Liberalism is no angel, at least not in its current state. Thus, while I remain unconvinced that liberalism's health is as terminal as Milbank and Pabst seem to be convinced that it is, I accept that the patient is seriously ill. What is at stake is an accurate diagnosis and an effective treatment. *The Politics of Virtue* represents a substantive contribution to both, and one which deserves to be read and discussed widely. I do, however, question whether Milbank and Pabst have correctly diagnosed the disease in this case. They describe the symptoms with great lucidity and perspicacity. But is liberalism itself the disease, as they contend, or is it rather infected with a foreign disease? This is the crucial question. There is a possibility that what Milbank and Pabst diagnose as liberal disease is actually itself early-onset post-liberalism, in which case a good deal of caution is in order before we enthusiastically welcome the post-liberal future of humanity.

---

17. Chesterton, *Orthodoxy*, 22.

Political Anthropology and the Post-Liberal Future

There appears to be a consensus that illiberal (post-liberal?) forces are on the rise globally, whether in the form of "neo-fascism"—described by Milbank and Pabst as "travestied post-liberalism"—or the increasingly censorious authoritarianism of latter-day progressive identity politics. Are these the inevitable product of liberalism or the very essence of what is killing liberalism? Milbank and Pabst's post-liberal political vision offers some attractive and worthwhile proposals for improving and humanizing our ailing political culture. But I believe it is too early to pronounce the death of liberalism and to vest our faith in the rise of a virtuous post-liberal phoenix. Rather, we should expend every effort in boosting the immune system of liberalism in an effort to inoculate it from the internal and external threat of illiberalism.

12

In Defense of Politics[1]

INTRODUCTION

IN AN AGE IN which the degeneration of politicians, political institutions, and political culture—let's call it "politics"—is now an article of faith, a defense of said politics sounds unfashionable at best, and insolent at worst. I contend that much of the widespread negative evaluation of Western politics lacks an explicit, consistent, or even discernible set of objective criteria upon which to support and substantiate its negative verdict. As a corollary, I contend that the prevalent negative criticism of politics lacks an objective measure by which to convincingly substantiate the premise of political degeneration. Such claims are often dependent on subjective readings of history and posited political trajectories. The defense of politics I wish to mount, then, is actually a type criticism. At risk of gross inelegance, it is a critique of political critique.

For the sake of clarification, I do not embark on a defense of the quality, integrity, or competence of the existing class of politicians and their parties, nor the institutions that mediate their political activity. Moreover, the reader can take it for granted that I recognize the legitimacy of political criticism and the vital

---

1. Originally published as "In Defense of Politics," *The New Polis*.

In Defense of Politics

function it plays in a healthy democracy. I further accept that particular protagonists in the current political arena are liable to criticism, and in many cases have earned legitimate censure. In this vein, I do not wish to argue that the current state of Western politics is laudable or good. My critique of the prevailing negative assessment of politics deliberately leaves open the possibility that we do indeed find ourselves in the midst of precipitous political degeneration, as I indicated in the previous chapter.

What I do claim is that those preaching political degeneration all-too infrequently take into consideration the natural constraints that delimit the possibilities of human collective action, and that these constraints consequently ought to moderate our political criticism. The essence of my defense of politics is that political criticism is often poorly grounded in realism. My contention is that the objective criteria required for valid political criticism must be feasible and realistic in light of the natural constraints on human political action.

Below I discuss three significant natural constrains that constitute grounds for tempering (putting on a more realistic footing) the prevalent negative judgments about the state and nature of our current politics. I refer to these as "the transcendence of reality," "the constraints of biology," and "the constraints of human nature."

THE TRANSCENDENCE OF REALITY

Reality as we humans experience it is fundamentally transcendent. This truth has recently come into stark relief through the digital revolution which has made accessible in ways previously unimagined mountains of data, theories, argument, testimony, opinion, and artistic expression—let's call it "knowledge"—that overwhelms mortal minds. Even controlling for the detritus that assaults our senses daily through multiple digital orifices, the sheer weight of valuable intellectual knowledge that is now available and that one would have to absorb in order to even begin to build something resembling a picture of reality transcends the intellectual capacity of any single human mind. Knowledge further transcends the finitude and temporality of individual human lives. Even if a single human mind were capable of consuming and digesting the totality of human knowledge, it would not find the time to do so. Moreover, knowledge is often incomplete, inconsistent, and contested, even amongst those boasting expertise.

Politics, as a quintessentially human activity, is highly constrained by the transcendence of knowledge. That is to say that no single political actor or group of actors working in concert (political party, institution, etc.) can possibly hope to acquire and assess all relevant knowledge in relation to a particular decision or course of action. Often, even the essential facts surrounding a necessary and urgent decision or course of action are lacking or are in dispute. No mortal political actor, therefore, acts with full visibility and full comprehension of the dynamic and complex network of variables that constitutes and shapes the political context in which political action must be undertaken.[2] Conservatism (at least in its traditional philosophical form) has generally done a better job of absorbing this insight than its rivals on the other side of the ledger. Burke, for example, "doubt[ed] whether the history of mankind is yet complete enough, if ever it can be so, to furnish grounds for a sure theory on the internal causes which necessarily affect the fortune of State."[3] He did not deny that such causes are in operation. He simply found them to be "infinitely uncertain" and "obscure."[4] Interestingly, awareness of the transcendent nature of reality can be discerned in the writing of the Apostle Paul: "For we know only in part, and we prophesy only in part; but when the complete comes, the partial will come to an end . . . For now we see in a mirror, dimly" (1 Cor 13:9–12).

---

2. MacIntyre identifies four sources of "systematic unpredictability in human affairs." They are "radical conceptual innovation," "the unpredictability of certain . . . future actions by each agent individually . . . in the social world," "the game-theoretic character of social life," and "pure contingency," to the extent that "trivial contingencies can powerfully influence the outcome of great events." MacIntyre, *After Virtue*, 89–95.

3. Burke, *Revolutionary Writings*, 254.

4. Burke, *Revolutionary Writings*, 254.

In Defense of Politics

It is not only political actors who are constrained by the partial and who see in a mirror dimly. Their critics too are hamstrung by incomplete visibility of all relevant data, as well as comprehension of all relevant variables, not to mention the complex interaction of those variables, particularly on the international stage where one finds a coterie of independent and sometimes mercurial actors (think Kim Jong-un and Donald Trump alike). Yet critics embark on political criticism as though reality were complete and not seen dimly through a mirror, utterly unforgiving of the natural constraints that the transcendence of reality imposes on even the most capable political actors.

The partial nature of our access to reality is a primary reason that good people seeking to realize the political good can be so tragically captive to error. It is also a reason why politics is perpetually an arena of contest rather than consensus. Partial access to reality opens the door to conflicting views of that reality and consequently to mutually exclusive political visions promising the same political good. The unbridgeable transcendence of reality ought to moderate the ideal politics against which many of us tacitly judge *actual* politics.

THE CONSTRAINTS OF BIOLOGY

Human biology is also a significant constraint on politics. Take communication as an example. Humans can only communicate with a finite number of other humans at any one time and in any single period (however defined). Modern communication technologies have certainly made it easier to communicate with ever greater numbers of people, but political actors are still constrained by the physical limits on communication. A political actor can only participate in so many meetings in a day. They can only make so many telephone calls. There is even a limit to how many tweets, no matter how profound or inane, one can physically send in a day while engaging in other duties. Furthermore, a not-insignificant amount of time must be spent attending to human physical needs, like sleep and nutrition, though many political actors valiantly wage a futile war against both.

It follows, then, that no political actor can hope to consult and communicate with all constituents and relevant experts, officials, colleagues, and organizations in all circumstances. Communication and consultation are therefore partial, which is to say constrained, in the same way that the acquisition and absorption of relevant and accurate information is. The list of biological constraints is expansive: the inability to be physically present in multiple locations at once, the time it takes to travel long distances, the inability to execute multiple complex tasks at the same time, or simply the time it takes to draft, check, and clear important documents. Yet some criticism of politics fails to sufficiently take into consideration the natural constraints on political action imposed by human biology and the linear nature of our time-bound physical existence.

The constraints of human biology should therefore also be factored into the development of objective criteria against which *actual* politics is judged. Like the transcendence of reality, the constraints of human biology are a regular cause of political failure, even if in the somewhat mundane sense of the inability of tired, overworked political actors with stressed personal relationships to perform optimally in their political roles.

THE CONSTRAINTS OF HUMAN NATURE

The essence of politics is people, not systems and laws. The latter cannot exist, indeed have no meaning, in the absence of the people who create them, utilize them, and in turn are affected by them. There is unending debate about human nature, particularly in relation to its potential and limitations. Debates aside, we all learn sooner or later that humans are far from perfect creatures. Thus, in addition to having to contend with extrinsic constraints on their political activity, humans also confront intrinsic constraints that retard their political effectiveness: "For out of the heart come evil intentions, murder, adultery, fornication, theft, false witness, slander" (Matt 15:19).

James Madison wisely observed that, "if men were angels no government would be necessary."[5] One could add as a corollary that, "if men were angels, government would be perfect." There is simply no conceivable way to prevent the talented but malevolent, or the well-intentioned but incompetent, from entering the political fray. Moreover, there is no realistic way to ensure that the good and the intelligent never make bad political decisions. Nor to ensure that they never succumb to common human temptations: jealousy, spite, lust, greed, pride, vanity, arrogance, narcissism. As Lord Acton famously remarked, "power tends to corrupt and absolute power corrupts absolutely. Great men are almost always bad men."[6] So in addition to the natural constraints of human biology discussed above, one must add the natural constraints imposed by human nature, and the way that what used to be known as human "appetites" constrain what humans are capable of in the context of collaborative endeavors.

And still, we continue to routinely succumb to one of two temptations that betray a blindness to the constraining effects of human nature on politics. On the one hand we continue to invest heroic hope in political messiahs beyond all reason in light of the biological and psychological limitations of human beings, as well as the fundamental transcendence of (political) reality. On the other hand, we then crucify political actors for daring to fall short of the impossible hopes we invest in them, as if we truly expected our affairs to be governed by angels.

CONCLUSION

I have contended that pessimistic assessments of the current state of Western politics all too often lack an explicit, objective, and realistic set of criteria by which to substantiate such pronouncements.

---

5. Madison, "Federalist Papers."
6. Dalberg, "Acton–Creighton Correspondence."

Much political criticism tacitly assumes an ideal political reality against which actual political performance can be judged. But this ideal is often left undefined. Moreover, it often operates entirely unbounded by the natural constraints that shape politics. There is perhaps no greater evidence of the natural constraints on politics, and the folly of ignoring them, than the uncanny ability of revolutionary utopias to resemble the regimes they replace. Living in the wake of the French Revolution, Alexis de Tocqueville was surprised to learn just how much continuity there in fact was between the new and the *ancien régime*.[7]

George Orwell understood that which bemused Tocqueville. In his famous political novel, *Animal Farm*, the pigs ultimately take up residence in the farmhouse and assume the role of the despised and deposed humans. For at the end of the day, the farm was still a farm and there is a finite number of ways to run a farm. The fact of the matter is that politics is delimited by nature (in the widest sense). It is neither a tabula rasa nor a realm of infinite possibility. This is not a new insight. Aristotle already understood perfectly well in the fourth century BC that there are a finite number of ways to apportion power in any political association: rule by one, rule by few, rule by many.[8] This insight led Hannah Arendt to wryly observe that "not a single novel form of government has been added for 2,500 years."[9]

I do not stand against political criticism, per se. It indisputably performs a vital function in service of our freedom and political well-being. Indeed, I have engaged in a type of (theo)political criticism throughout this book. Yet, if political criticism is to play a positive and constructive role in our contemporary political life, particularly in an age of discontent, then it must be anchored in much greater realism about the natural constraints on human cooperation. I therefore stand with the fallen humans seeking to perform tasks better suited to angels. I defend them (at least the best of them) from criticism that measures them against the impossible

7. de Tocqueville, *Ancien Régime and the Revolution*, 9.
8. See Aristotle, *Politics*, book II.
9. Arendt, "Great Tradition: I," 715.

standard of an undefined ideal politics that is perpetually promised but yet to materialize. And with the Apostle Paul, I offer "prayers, intercessions, supplications, *and* thanksgivings . . . for kings and all who are in high positions, so that we may lead a quiet and peaceable life in all godliness and dignity" (1 Tim 2:1–2).[10]

---

10. Emphasis mine.

Bibliography

Abramovitch, Seth. "Donald Trump Viral Baby Photo: The Photographer Speaks." *The Hollywood Reporter.* August 25, 2015. https://www.hollywoodreporter.com/news/donald-trump-viral-baby-photo-817567.

The American Conservative Union. "What We Believe." https://conservative.org/what-we-believe.

The American Presidency Project. "2016 Republican Party Platform." http://www.presidency.ucsb.edu/ws/index.php?pid=117718.

Arendt, Hannah. "The Great Tradition: I. Law and Power." *Social Research* 74.3 (2007) 713–26.

Aristotle. *The Athenian Constitution.* Translated by H. Rackham. Cambridge, MA: Harvard University Press, 1952.

———. *Politics.* Translated by H. Rackham. Cambridge, MA: Harvard University Press, 1934.

Augustine. *Concerning the City of God Against the Pagans.* Translated by Henry Bettenson, with a new introduction by G. R. Evans. London: Penguin, 2003.

Bacon, Edwin. "Why Exactly Does Political Theology Need to Become a "Real Discipline"?—A Response to Jonathan Cole." *The Political Theology Network,* October 11, 2016. https://politicaltheology.com/why-exactly-does-political-theology-need-to-become-a-real-discpline-a-response-to-jonathan-cole-edwin-bacon/.

Bakunin, Michael. "The Political Theology of Mazzini." In *Michael Bakunin: Selected Writings.* Edited and introduced by Arthur Lehning, translated from the French by Steven Cox and translated from the Russian by Olive Stevens, 214–31. London: Jonathan Cape, 1973.

Barth, Karl. "The Christian Community and the Civil Community." In *Community, State, and Church: Three Essays,* 149–89. Gloucester, MA: Peter Smith, 1968.

Burke, Edmund. *Revolutionary Writings: Reflections on the Revolution in France and the First Letter on a Regicide Peace.* Edited by Iain Hampsher-Monk. Cambridge: Cambridge University Press, 2014.

Calvin, John. "On Civil Government." In *On God and Political Duty.* Edited by John T. McNeil, 44–82. Indianapolis: Bobbs-Merill, 1956.

Bibliography

Canning, Joseph. *A History of Medieval Political Thought 300–1450.* London: Routledge, 1996.

Cavanaugh, William T. *Theopolitical Imagination: Discovering the Liturgy as a Political Act in an Age of Global Consumerism.* London: Bloomsbury T & T Clark, 2002.

Chesterton, Gilbert K. *Orthodoxy.* London: John Lane, 1909.

Cillizza, Chris. "Let's Break Down This Amazing Donald Trump Picture from his Alabama Rally." *The Washington Post*, August 24, 2015. https://www.washingtonpost.com/news/the-fix/wp/2015/08/24/breaking-down-this-amazing-donald-trump-picture-from-his-alabama-rally/?utm_term=.982ec80185fe.

Cole, Jonathan. "The Art of Political Theology—Finding the Right Definition and the Proper Set of Questions." *The Political Theology Network*, March 8, 2017. https://politicaltheology.com/the-art-of-political-theology-finding-the-right-definition-and-the-proper-set-of-questions-jonathan-cole/.

———. "A Calvinist Take On Why Evangelicals Support Donald Trump." *The Political Theology Network*, December 12, 2017. https://politicaltheology.com/a-calvinist-take-on-why-evangelicals-support-donald-trump-jonathan-cole/.

———. "Carl Schmitt and the True German Origins of Political Theology." *The New Polis*, September 11, 2018. http://thenewpolis.com/2018/09/11/carl-schmitt-and-the-true-german-origins-of-political-theology-jonathan-cole/.

———. "Christian Political Theology Needs to Grow up and Become a Real Discipline." *The Political Theology Network*, October 5, 2016. https://politicaltheology.com/christian-political-theology-needs-to-grow-up-and-become-a-real-discipline-jonathan-cole/.

———. "Conservatives' Core Values Not As Theologically Grounded As Many Believe." *The Political Theology Network*, May 31, 2017. https://politicaltheology.com/conservatives-core-values-not-as-theologically-grounded-as-many-believe-jonathan-cole/.

———. ""Delegated Divine Rule"—On Hobbes And The Origins Of Political Theology." *The Political Theology Network*, October 18, 2017. https://politicaltheology.com/delegated-divine-rule-on-hobbes-and-the-origins-of-political-theology-jonathan-cole/.

———. "In Defense of Politics." *The New Polis*, April 1, 2018. http://thenewpolis.com/2018/04/01/in-defense-of-politics-jonathan-cole/.

———. "John Howard Yoder and the New Prospects For a Christian Politics." *The Political Theology Network*, February 14, 2017. https://politicaltheology.com/john-howard-yoder-and-the-new-prospects-for-a-christian-politics-jonathan-cole/.

———. "Political Anthropology and the Post-Liberal Future. *The Political Theology Network*, September 5, 2017. https://politicaltheology.com/political-anthropology-and-the-post-liberal-future-jonathan-cole/.

———. "Political Theology Must Be Engaged More Profoundly With Political Philosophy." *The Political Theology Network*, May 4, 2017. https://politicaltheology.com/political-theology-must-be-engaged-more-profoundly-with-political-philosophy-jonathan-cole/.

———. "The Problem with "Christian" Political Theology—It's Greek, Not Christian." *The New Polis*, July 11, 2018. http://thenewpolis.com/2018/07/11/the-problem-with-christian-political-theology-its-greek-not-christian-jonathan-cole/.

———. ""Thank You Lord Jesus For President Trump"—Apostolic Theology and the Evangelical Vote." *The Political Theology Network*, January 5, 2017. https://politicaltheology.com/thank-you-lord-jesus-for-president-trump-apostolic-theology-and-the-evangelical-vote-jonathan-cole/.

Dalberg, John Emerich Edward. "Acton–Creighton Correspondence." Online Library of Liberty. http://oll.libertyfund.org/titles/acton-acton-creighton-correspondence.

Day, Katie, and Sebastian Kim, eds. *A Companion to Public Theology*. Leiden: Brill, 2017.

de Tocqueville, Alexis. *The Ancien Régime and the Revolution*. Translated by Gerald Bevan. London: Penguin, 2008.

de Vries, Hent, ed. "Introduction: Before, Around, and Beyond the Theologico-Political." In *Political Theologies: Public Religions in a Post-Secular World*, edited by Hent de Vries and Laurence E. Sullivan, 1–88. New York: Fordham University Press, 2006.

Derrida, Jacques. *The Beast and the Sovereign*, Volume 2. Translated by Geoffrey Bennington. Chicago: University of Chicago Press, 2011.

———. "Force of Law: The 'Mystical Foundation of Authority.'" In Jacques Derrida, *Acts of Religion*, edited by Gil Andijar, 228–98. New York: Routledge, 2002.

———. *Politics of Friendship*. Translated by George Collins. London: Verso, 1997.

———. *Rogues: Two Essays on Reason*. Translated by Pascale-Anne Brault and Michael Naas. Stanford: Stanford University Press, 2004.

———. *Specters of Marx: The State of the Debt, the Work of Mourning and the New International*. Translated by Peggy Kamuf. Abingdon: Routledge, 2006.

Dooyeweerd, Herman. *The Christian Idea of the State*. Translated by John Kraay. New Jersey: Craig, 1968.

Ellul, Jacques. *Anarchy and Christianity*. Translated by Geoffrey W. Bromiley. Grand Rapids, MI: Eerdmans, 1991.

Family Research Council. "FAQs." https://www.frc.org/faqs.

Finnis, John. *Natural Law and Natural Rights*. Oxford: Oxford University Press, 2011.

Fukuyama, Francis. *The End of History and the Last Man*. London: Hamilton, 1992.

Bibliography

Gottwald, Norman K. *The Politics of Ancient Israel*. Louisville: Westminster John Knox, 2001.

Gutiérrez, Gustavo. *A Theology of Liberation: History, Politics, and Salvation*. Translated by Sister Caridad Inda and John Eagleson. London: SCM, 2001.

Habermas, Jürgen. *Legitimation Crisis*. Translated by Thomas McCarthy. London: Heinemann, 1976.

Hauerwas, Stanley. *After Christendom? How the Church is to Behave if Freedom, Justice, and a Christian Nation are Bad Ideas*. Nashville: Abingdon, 1991.

Hauerwas, Stanley, and William H. Willimon. *Resident Aliens: A Provocative Christian Assessment of Culture and Ministry for People who Know that Something is Wrong*. Nashville: Abingdon, 1989.

Hay, Colin. "Neither Real Nor Fictitious But 'As if Real'? A Political Ontology of the State." *The British Journal of Sociology* 65 (2014) 459–80.

Hayward, Jack. "British Approaches to Politics: The Dawn of a Self-Deprecating Discipline." In *The British Study of Politics in the Twentieth Century*, edited by Jack Hayward et al., 1–35. Oxford: Oxford University Press, 1999.

Herrero, Montserrat. "Carl Schmitt's Political Theology: The Magic of a Phrase." In *Political Theology in Medieval and Early Modern Europe: Discourses, Rites, and Representations*, edited by Jaume Aurelle et al., 23–41. Turnhout: Brepols, 2017.

———. "On Political Theology: The Hidden Dialogue between C. Schmitt and Ernst H. Kantorowicz in *The King's Two Bodies*." *History of European Ideas* 41 (2015) 1164–1177.

Hobbes, Thomas. *Leviathan*. Edited by C. B. Macpherson. London: Penguin, 1985.

Holmes, Michael W. "Introduction" to *The Epistle to Diognetus and the Fragment of Quadratus*. In *The Apostolic Fathers: Greek Texts and English Translations*, edited and translated by Michael W. Holmes, 686–721. Grand Rapids, MI: Baker Academic, 2007.

Holmes, Michael W., ed. and trans. *First Clement*. In *The Apostolic Fathers Greek Texts and English Translations*, 44–131. Grand Rapids, MI: Baker Academic, 2007.

———. *The Martyrdom of Polycarp*. In *The Apostolic Fathers Greek Texts and English Translations*, 306–33. Grand Rapids, MI: Baker Academic, 2007.

Hovey, Craig, and Elizabeth Phillips, eds. *The Cambridge Companion to Political Theology*. Cambridge: Cambridge University Press, 2015.

Kantorowicz, Ernst Hartwig. "Deus Per Naturam, Deus Per Gratiam: A Note on Mediaeval Political Theology." *The Harvard Theological Review* 45 (1952) 253–77.

———. *The King's Two Bodies: A Study in Mediaeval Political Theology*. Princeton: Princeton University Press, 1957.

Kee, Alistair, ed. *A Reader in Political Theology*. London: SCM, 1974.

Kirk, Russell. *The Conservative Mind: From Burke to Eliot*. New Jersey: Gateway Editions, 2001.

———. *The Sword of Imagination: Memoirs of a Half-Century of Literary Conflict*. Grand Rapids, MI: Eerdmans, 1995.
Kuyper, Abraham. *Lectures on Calvinism*. Grand Rapids, MI: Eerdmans, 1931.
Lilla, Mark. *The Stillborn God: Religion, Politics, and the Modern West*. New York: Knopf, 2007.
Lloyd, Vincent, and David True. "What Political Theology Could Be." *Political Theology* 17 (2016) 505–6.
Luther, Martin. "On Secular Government." In *Luther and Calvin on Secular Authority*, edited and translated by Harro Höpfl, 3–43. Cambridge: Cambridge University Press, 1991.
MacIntyre, Alasdair. *After Virtue: A Study in Moral Theory*. London: Duckworth, 1981.
Macquarie Complete Australian Dictionary. Multimedia application. 6th ed. Pan Macmillan Australia, 2015.
Madison, James. "The Federalist Papers: No. 51." http://avalon.law.yale.edu/18th_century/fed51.asp.
McLean, Iain, and Alistair McMillan, eds. "Government." *Oxford Concise Dictionary of Politics*. Oxford: Oxford University Press, 2009.
Metz, John B. "Religion and Society in the Light of a Political Theology." *The Harvard Theological Review* 61 (1968) 507–23.
———. *Theology of the World*. Translated by William Glen-Doepel. New York: Herder and Herder, 1969.
Micklem, Nathaniel. *The Theology of Politics*. London: Religious Book Club, 1941.
Midgley, Louis C. "Ultimate Concern and Politics: A Critical Examination of Paul Tillich's Political Theology." *The Western Political Quarterly* 20 (1967) 31–50.
Migliore, Daniel L. "Biblical Eschatology and Political Hermeneutics." *Theology Today* 26 (1969) 116–32.
Milbank, John, and Adrian Pabst. *The Politics of Virtue: Post-Liberalism and the Human Future*. London: Rowman & Littlefield, 2016.
Moltmann, Jürgen. "Political Theology." *Theology Today* 28 (1971) 6–23.
Oakley, Francis. "Jacobean Political Theology: The Absolute and Ordinary Powers of the King." *Journal of the History of Ideas* 29 (1968) 323–46.
Obermann, Julian. "Political Theology in Early Islam: Ḥasan Al-Baṣrī's Treatise on Qadar." *Journal of the American Oriental Society* 55 (1935) 138–62.
O'Donovan, Oliver. *The Desire of the Nations: Rediscovering the Roots of Political Theology*. Cambridge: Cambridge University Press, 1996.
———. *The Ways of Judgment: The Bampton Lectures, 2003*. Grand Rapids, MI: Eerdmans, 2005.
Orwell, George. *Animal Farm*. London: Penguin, 2008.
Papanikolaou, Aristotle. *The Mystical as Political: Democracy and Non-Radical Orthodoxy*. Notre Dame: Notre Dame University Press, 2014.
Phillips, Elizabeth. *Political Theology: A Guide for the Perplexed*. London: T & T Clark, 2012.

Bibliography

Popper, Karl R. *Unended Quest: An Intellectual Autobiography*. Glasgow: Collins, 1976.

Postman, Neil. *Amusing Ourselves to Death: Public Discourse in the Age of Showbusiness*. New York: Penguin, 1985.

Proudhon, Pierre-Joseph. *What is Property? An Inquiry into the Principle of Right and of Government*. http://www.gutenberg.org/files/360/360-h/360-h.htm.

Ramsey, Paul. *Basic Christian Ethics*. Louisville: Westminster/John Knox, 1993.

Raschke, Carl A. *Force of God: Political Theology and the Crisis of Liberal Democracy*. New York: Columbia University Press, 2015.

Raz, Joseph. "Authority and Justification." *Philosophy & Public Affairs* 14 (1985) 3–29.

Schmemann, Alexander. *Church, World, Mission: Reflections on Orthodoxy in the West*. New York: St Vladimir's Seminary, 1979.

Schmitt, Carl. *Political Theology: Four Chapters on the Concept of Sovereignty*. Translated with an introduction by George Schwab, with a foreword by Tracy B. Strong. Chicago: University of Chicago Press, 2005.

———. *Political Theology II: The Myth of the Closure of Any Political Theology*. Translated with an introduction by Michael Hoelzl and Graham Ward. Malden, MA: Polity, 2008. Kindle edition.

Scott, Peter, and William T. Cavanaugh, eds. *The Blackwell Companion to Political Theology*. Oxford: Blackwell, 2004.

Scruton, Roger. *The Meaning of Conservatism*. Basingstoke, Hampshire: Palgrave Macmillan, 2001.

Shepsle, Kenneth A. *Analyzing Politics: Rationality, Behavior, and Institutions*. New York: W. W. Norton, 2010.

Sherwood, Harriet. "The Chosen One? The New Film That Claims Trump's Election Was an Act of God." *The Guardian*, October 3, 2018. https://www.theguardian.com/us-news/2018/oct/03/the-trump-prophecy-film-god-election-mark-taylor.

Smith, Gregory A. "Among White Evangelicals, Regular Churchgoers Are the Most Supportive of Trump." *Pew Research Center*, April 26, 2017. http://www.pewresearch.org/fact-tank/2017/04/26/among-white-evangelicals-regular-churchgoers-are-the-most-supportive-of-trump/.

Smith, Gregory A., and Jessica Martínez. "How the Faithful Voted: A Preliminary 2016 Analysis." *Pew Research Center*, November 9, 2016. http://www.pewresearch.org/fact-tank/2016/11/09/how-the-faithful-voted-a-preliminary-2016-analysis/.

Soelle, Dorothee. *Political Theology*. Translated by John Shelley. Philadelphia: Fortress, 1974.

Spinoza, Baruch. *Tractatus Theologico-Politicus*. Translated by S. Shirley. Introduction by B.S. Gregory. Leiden: Brill, 1997.

Stoeckl, Kristina, et al., eds. *Political Theologies in Orthodox Christianity: Common Challenges—Divergent Positions*. London: T & T Clark, 2018.

Bibliography

Tharoor, Ishaan. "The man who declared the 'end of history' fears for democracy's future." *The Washington Post*, February 9, 2017. https://www.washingtonpost.com/news/worldviews/wp/2017/02/09/the-man-who-declared-the-end-of-history-fears-for-democracys-future/?utm_term=.a362e8535baf.

USA Today. "Billy Graham's Son: God Put Trump in Office." *USA Today*, May 4, 2018. https://www.usatoday.com/videos/news/nation/2018/05/04/billy-grahams-son-god-put-trump-office/34543485/.

Walzer, Michael. *In God's Shadow: Politics in the Hebrew Bible*. New Haven: Yale University Press, 2012.

Whitehouse.gov. "Presidential Executive Order Promoting Free Speech and Religious Liberty." https://www.whitehouse.gov/presidential-actions/presidential-executive-order-promoting-free-speech-religious-liberty/.

Winthrop, John. "A Model of Christian Charity." https://www.winthropsociety.com/doc_charity.php.

Wolff, Robert P. "The Conflict between Authority and Autonomy." In *Authority*, edited by Joseph Raz, 20–31. Oxford: Basil Blackwell, 1990.

Wolterstorff, Nicholas. *The Mighty and the Almighty: An Essay in Political Theology*. Cambridge: Cambridge University Press, 2012.

Worden, Blair. *The English Civil Wars, 1640–1660*. London: Orion, 2009. iBooks.

Yannaras, Christos. Ἡ ἀπανθρωπία τοῦ δικαιώματος [*The Inhumanity of Rights*]. Athens: Domos, 1998.

———. "Συνεπάγεται αχρείωση ο αφελληνισμός" [De-Hellenization Implies Degeneration]. *Kathimerini*, August 10, 2014. http://www.kathimerini.gr/779516/opinion/epikairothta/politikh/synepagetai-axreiwsh-o-afellhnismos.

Yoder, John Howard. *The Christian Witness to the State*. Scottdale: Herald, 2002.

———. *The Politics of Jesus: Vicit Agnus Noster*. Grand Rapids, MI: Eerdmans, 1994.

Subject Index

America/American, x, xvii, 23, 27,
  32–33, 36, 55–60, 62, 65–73,
  76–77
American Conservative Union, The,
  69–70
American democracy. See
  democracy.
Americans for Constitutional
  Liberty (The Conservative
  Caucus), 69
anarchism, 2
  Christian, 76, 80, 82–84
anarchist, xxiii, 43, 80, 82
anthropology/anthropological, 46,
  71, 91–92
  biblical, 92
  Christian, 35
  comparative, 12
  foundational, 91
  Hobbes's, 47
  liberalism's, 92
  pessimistic, 88, 90–91
  political, 86, 90–91
atheism/atheist, xxiii–xxiv, 3, 44, 75
authoritarianism/authoritarian, x,
  xii, 93
authority, ix, x, xii, 1, 3, 12, 17, 40,
  42, 49, 57, 79–81
  divine, 64
  God's, 64, 66–67
  legal, 22, 51

legislative, 51
legitimate, 58
political, xv, xxiv, 2–4, 21, 34,
  39–43, 52, 64, 79–82, 84–85
theological, 71

Bible/biblical, xi, xiv, xxiv–xxvi,
  1, 3–5, 8–9, 14, 18, 30–34,
  42–43, 46, 48–50, 52–53,
  57–58, 60, 64, 71–72, 74–75,
  77–78, 80–83, 92
Byzantium/Byzantine, 7, 32–33, 35

Catholicism/Catholic, x, 9, 23–24,
  63–64, 68–69, 75
Christ. See Jesus.
Christendom, xvi, 7, 32–36
Christian Republic, 51
church, xi, xxiv–xxvi, 2–4, 6, 9–10,
  14–15, 18, 31, 35–36, 41, 50,
  57, 63, 68, 74–75, 78, 82–83
citizenship, 2, 5, 30
citizen
  Bible-reading, 60
  Christian, xvi, xxvii, 32–33
  inherent rights, 70
  jury, 31
  of liberal societies, 88
  sovereignty, 34
  Western, xxiv
conservatism, 68–69, 70–76, 96

Subject Index

conservative
  and liberal church, 36
  Christian, 74–75
  counterrevolutionary political thought, 22
  dissenters, 76
  judicial, 59
  movement, 68–69, 72, 75–76
  political agenda, 74
  political organizations, 69
  political philosophy, 73
  principles, 73
  speakers, 77
  theory of the state, 23
  values, 69, 74
  view of the family, 74
constitution
  American, 32, 71
  Athenian, 32
  of the church, 63
constitutional
  conception, 34
  corporatism, 89
  first principles, xii
  rights, 34
covenant/covenantal, xiv, xvi, xxv, 34, 40, 47–48, 51, 71
  Abrahamic, 48, 51
  Israel's, 42
creation, 2, 71, 73, 92
cross, 26, 78, 83–84
culture/cultural, ix, xv, 3, 12, 15, 34–35, 37, 86–87, 93–94

democracy/democratic, xii, 23, 31, 33–34, 36, 52, 64, 86, 95
  American, 36
  election/s, 57–36
  grass-roots, x
  liberal, 2, 7, 33, 36
  of Pericles, 17
Democratic party/Democratic, 59, 74, 77
devil, 67, 78, 81, 92

doctrine
  Christian, xxvii, 4, 48
  evangelical, xxvii
  of creation, 71, 73
  of *imitatio Christi*, 83
  of liberal sin, 92
  of original sin, 92
  of religion, 63
  of the kingdom of God, 52
  Orthodox, xxvii
  theological, xiv, xxv–xxvi, 4, 52–53, 75

Eagle Forum, 69
ecclesial. *See* church.
ecclesiastic. *See* church.
ecclesiological. *See* church.
economics/economic, ix–x, xvi, 12, 70, 87
  institutions, 89
  justice, 87
  neoliberal, ix
  theory, 72
economy, 86
  divine, 34
  global, xi
election/s, 58
  democratic, 57–59
  presidential, 58
  Trump's, 56
empire, 2, 83
  Christian, 32
  monarchical, 33
Enlightenment, 7
ethic
  communicative, x
  normative, 2
  social, 36
ethical, xv–xvi, 78
ethics
  Christian, 39
  political, 15, 26
  social, 27, 77
Europe, x–xi, 29

Subject Index

evangelicalism/evangelical, xviii, 55–58, 61–62, 65–68
evil, 51, 62, 67, 92, 98
exaltation, xxvi, 41–42, 84

fall/fallen, xxiii, 67, 75, 84, 92, 100
Family Research Council, 69–70
fascism, 2, 93
freedom/s, 54, 70–72, 78, 88, 90, 100
    created, 74
    economic, 70
    educational, 69
    from sin, 71
    from slavery, 72
    individual, 69, 70, 73–74
    of choice, 90
    personal, 72, 90
    political, 70
    positive, 88
    religious, 61, 66
FreedomWorks, 69
fundamentalism, xii

God, xviii, xxvi, 2–3, 12, 15, 22–23, 30, 32, 40, 42–43, 47–54, 56–60, 63–67, 70–73, 75, 78–79, 81–83, 85
governance, xv, 17–18
government, xviii, xxvii, 14–15, 17, 40–41, 47, 62–64, 67, 70, 72, 79, 81–82, 99–100
    Christian civil, 51
    civil, xviii, 50, 62–63, 66–67
    divine, 82
    limited, 69–70, 72–73
    secular, 54, 78
    theory of, 47
    tyrannical, 79
Greece/Greek, xiii–xvi, xxv, 5, 8, 30–37, 56

Heritage Foundation, The, 69
history, x, xviii, xxvi–xxvii, 3–4, 8, 14, 20, 22, 29, 34, 41, 43, 54, 82, 94, 96

Christian, 57
    end of, 86
    global, 60
    human, 2
    political, 7–9, 31, 59, 76
    recorded, 8
    sacred, 8
    salvation-, 41, 43
Holy Spirit, xxvi

identity politics, 93
illegitimacy, 79, 85
image-bearers. *See imago Dei.*
image of the creator. *See imago Dei.*
image of God. *See imago Dei.*
imago Dei, xxvi, 2, 64, 66, 71–73
incarnation, xxvi
institution, 15, 17, 38, 89–90, 94, 96
    economic, 89
    democratic, 31
    governing, 18
    political, 34

ISIS, 13–14, 17
Islam/Islamic, 8–9, 27, 66
Israel/Israelite, 7–8, 31–35, 40, 42, 50, 80–81

Jesus, xiv, 3, 26–27, 32, 53, 55–58, 71–72, 76–78, 80–84
Jews/Jewish, x, 5, 8, 62, 71, 78
John Birch Society, 69
judgment, xxv, 2–3, 16, 41, 47, 54, 59, 65, 95

kingdom, 31, 51, 83
    earthly/on earth, 50–51
    heavenly, xvii, 63, 67
    of Christ, xviii, 51, 62–3, 67
    of God, 50–52, 83
kingship, 2
    divine, xvi, 32–33, 42
    God's, 2, 40

Latin America, xi

Subject Index

law, xii, 2, 21–22, 39, 49, 63, 88, 98
  divine, 49, 51
  moral, 48–49
  natural/of nature, xvii, 48–50, 52–53
  positive, 49
  public, 22
leader
  anointed, 58
  moral character among, xviii
  political, xvii, 6, 57, 60
left
  and right, 32
  Christian, xiv, 77
  far, 79, 85
  radical, 85
  -right spectrum, 73, 77
  secular, 84
  socio-cultural liberalism of the, 87
  transformations on the, 77
  -wing, x
Leftist, 85
legitimacy/legitimate/legitimation/legitimating
  authority, 58, 81
  censure, 95
  command, 39–40
  concept of, 23
  crisis, ix–x, xv, 86
  governing authorities, 79
  issues of, xvi
  legal authority and, 22
  matters of, xviii
  models of, xv
  of political criticism, 94
  political authority, 39, 41, 79–83
  political order, ix, xxiv–xv
  pressures of, ix
  principles of, x
  state as, 43
liberalism/liberal
  and post-liberalism, 88–89
  anthropology of, 90–92
  as a philosophy, 86
  church, 36
  crisis, 86
  critique of, 87
  death of, 93
  democracy, 91,
  dogma, 86
  false ontology, 91
  health of, 87
  ideas and institutions, 90
  order/s, 88
  politics, 86
  post-liberal alternative to, 87
  sin, 92
  social-cultural, 87
  societies, 88, 90
  structural reality of, 88
  theory, 90
  tyranny, 58, 89
  universalism, 36
  world, 86, 89, 91
  Western, 36
liberal/s, xviii, 2
liberation theology, xi, 25
libertarian, 74
liberty
  negative, 88, 90
  political, 70
  positive, 88, 90
  religious, 65, 74

magistrate, 57–58, 64–66
  Christian, 64, 66
  civil, 64
Marxism/Marxist, ix–xi, xv–xvi
mediate, xiv, xxv, 40, 89, 94
medieval, 28, 33, 35
messiah/messianic/messianism, x–xi, 59, 99
monarchism/monarchy/monarch/monarchial, x, 23–24, 32–33, 50, 82
  Christian, x, 33
  Davidic, 40

Subject Index

hereditary, 2
Israelite, 51
theocratic, 82
tributary agrarian, 32–33

nation-state. *See* state.
nature
    delimited by, 100
    existence of man, reason, and, 53
    fallen, 67
    human, xxiii, 71, 90–91, 95, 98–99
    lawfulness of, 22
    law/s of, 48–49 53
    of men, 48
    principles of, 48
    reason and, 46
Nazism/Nazi, x–xi, 29
neoliberalism/neoliberal xv
    economics, ix
    reorganization of the global economy, xi
    world order, xiv
norm/normative, xiv, xvi, 1–3, 7–8, 19, 24, 28, 32–35, 40, 42–43, 82–84
North America, 17, 28

ontology, xxvi–xxvii, 19, 31, 90–91
order, 13, 23, 65, 79, 85
    created, 73
    divine, ix, 63
    institutional, 85
    liberal, ix, 88
    political, ix, xv, xvii, xxiv, 3, 8–9, 48, 53, 64, 85
    religious, 12
    Western liberal political, 32–35
    world, xiv, 86
Orthodox, xxvii, 7, 9, 35

philosophy
    counterrevolutionary, 21
    European, xi
    liberalism as a, 86
    of law, 39
    political, xxvii, 5, 12, 15, 27–28, 38–39, 41–46, 52, 73, 75
    schools, 38
political science, xxvii, 15, 37
policy, x, 1–2, 7, 16
polis, 5, 35
post-liberalism, 86–93
power 12–13, 15, 24, 41, 48–49, 57, 59, 63, 81, 87, 89, 99–100
    common, 47
    connections among those who participate in the political processes, xv
    Constantinian, 36
    demonic, 79
    God's sovereign, xvii, 48
    of Christ, 78
    of the cross, 83
    ontic, xii
    political, 81
    relations, xxvii
    sovereign, 48, 52, 64
    structural, 12
progressive, xi, 77, 93
providence/providential, xix, 18, 40–42, 50, 54, 60, 64
public theology, 15, 25

radical, xi, 22–23, 63, 77, 79, 81, 83–85, 89, 96
reason/rational/rationality/reasoning, xii–xiii, xvi–xvii, 39, 42–43, 46, 49–51, 53–54, 73
redemption/redemptive, 78–79, 92
religious, x–xii, xv, xvii, xix, 3, 12, 14, 51, 61, 65–66, 68, 74–75
republican, xvii
Republican party/Republican, 59–60, 68–74, 76
resurrection, 32, 84
revolution/revolutionary, xiv, xxv, 77–84, 95, 100

Subject Index

right
  both left and, 32
  Christian, 77
  right-leaning libertarians, 74
  left-right spectrum, 73, 77
  the economic-political
    liberalism of the, 87
  transformations on the, 77
right/s
  civil, 71
  constitutional, 34
  divine, 32
  execution of, 41
  inalienable, 70
  individual, 71–72
  inherent, 70
  of sovereign power, 48
  political, 71
  religious, 65
  to accumulate private wealth, 74
  to bear arms, 72
  to educate children, 73
  to exist, 4
  to homeschool, 72

salvation, 12, 25, 35, 50–51, 83–84
Satan. See devil.
science, xxiii, xxv
Scripture/scriptural. See Bible/
  biblical.
secular 75, 77–79, 83–84
  account of political order, 53
  appropriation of Hobbes, 52
  contractarian theories, 43
  counterparts, 55
  ethics, 15
  governance, 18
  government/s, 54, 78–79
  ideological fashions, 77
  left, 84
  philosophers, xiii, xviii,
  political authority, 79, 83
  political ideologies, xiii
  political philosophy, xviii, 5,
    38–39, 44, 67, 75

political science, xxvii
political thought/thinkers, 5, 9
politics, 35
post-theological age, xvii
spiritual and the, 62
theorists, xxvi
secularization/secularize, xvii, 22, 28
sin, 64, 71–72, 78, 84, 92
social, ix, xiv–xv, 12, 15, 26, 36, 71,
    87
  change, 27
  environment, 71
  ethics, 27, 77
  good, 72, 85
  life, 4, 96
  meaning, 78
  movement, 3
  peace, 64
  phenomenona, 42
  reciprocity, 87
  relations, xxvii
  transformation, x
  world, 25, 96
socialism, 2
social media, xiii, xxiii, 56
sociology/sociological, 12–13, 38, 71
sovereignty/sovereign, ix–x, xii,
    20–23, 47–52, 54, 79
  divine, xxvi, 52
  God's/of God, xvi–xvii, 48
  national, 69, 72–73
  of Satan, 78
  power, 52, 64
  state, ix, xii, xvii, 13–15, 17, 21–24,
    36, 43, 60, 78, 80, 82, 90, 96
Supreme Court, 59, 61, 65, 73

telos/teleology, xiii, xxv–xxvii, 19, 31

UN, 13–14, 17
United States of America. See
  America.

Weimar Republic, ix

116

Author Index

Acton, Lord, 99
Agamben, Giorgio, 44
Aristotle, xii, 32, 100
Augustine, 15

Badiou, Alain, xiii
Bakunin, Mikhail, 20
Benjamin, Walter, x
Buckley, William F., 69
Burke, Edmund, 20, 96

Calvin, John, xviii, 57–58, 61–67
Cavanaugh, William T., 11, 13, 73
Chesterton, G.K., 92
Clement, 83
Clinton, Bill, 20
Clinton, Hillary, 66, 68
Cromwell, Oliver, 51

Dawkins, Richard, 44
Derrida, Jacques, xi–xiii
Diognetus, 16

Ellul, Jacques, 76, 80–85

Foucault, Michel, xv

Gottwald, Norman K., 32
Graham, Franklin, 56
Gutiérrez, Gustavo, xi, 25

Habermas, Jürgen, ix–x
Hauerwas, Stanley, 35–37
Hayward, Jack, xxiii
Herrero, Montserrat, 20, 24, 26, 29
Hobbes, Thomas, xvii, 46–54, 62, 90–91
Hoelzl, Michael, 29
Hovey, Craig, 13

Kantorowicz, Ernst Harwig, 27–28
Kee, Alistair, 26
Kelsen, Hans, 23
Kirk, Russell, 69, 75

Leibniz, Gottfried Wilhelm, 23
Lilla, Mark, 52–54
Luther, Martin, 62

MacIntyre, Alasdair, 44, 96
Madison, James, 99
Marx, Karl, ix
Metz, Johann Baptist, x, 9, 24–26, 28–29
Migliore, Daniel L., 27
Milbank, John, 86–93
Moltmann, Jürgen, x, 26–29

Niebuhr, Reinhold, 9, 27

Obama, Barack, 58
Obermann, Julian, 27–28

Author Index

O'Donovan, Oliver, 8–9, 14, 17, 32, 34–42, 52, 54, 87, 90
Orwell, George, 100

Pabst, Adrian, 86–93
Paul, Apostle, 31, 57, 83, 92, 96, 101
Phillips, Elizabeth, 13
Plantinga, Alvin, 44
Polycarp, 83
Popper, Karl, 16
Proudhon, Pierre-Joseph, xxiii
Ramsey, Paul, 64

Raz, Joseph, 38–43
Rousseau, Jean-Jacques, xii

Schmitt, Carl, ix–xiii, xv–xvi, 20–29
Schwab, George, 21
Scott, Peter, 11, 13
Scruton, Roger, 6
Segundo, Juan Luis, xi
Shepsle, Kenneth, 17

Soelle, Dorothee, 26, 28
Spinoza, Baruch, 20
Strong, Tracy, 21

Taylor, Charles, 44
Tocqueville, Alexis de, 100
Trump, Donald, xviii, 55–58, 60–62, 65–68, 76–77, 86, 97

Vries, Hent de, 12–13, 20

Walzer, Michael, 30–31
Ward, Graham, 29
Winthrop, John, 60
Wolff, Robert P., 43
Wolterstorff, Nicholas, 13–14, 44

Yannaras, Christos, 9, 35–37
Yoder, John Howard, 9, 27, 76–85

Žižek, Slavoj, xiii, 44

www.ingramcontent.com/pod-product-compliance
Lightning Source LLC
Chambersburg PA
CBHW072150160426
43197CB00012B/2323